IN
DEFENSE
OF
ELITISM

ALSO BY JOEL STEIN

Man Made: A Stupid Quest for Masculinity

IN DEFENSE OF ELITISM

WHY I'M BETTER THAN YOU AND
YOU'RE BETTER THAN SOMEONE
WHO DIDN'T BUY THIS BOOK

JOEL STEIN

GRAND CENTRAL
PUBLISHING

NEW YORK   BOSTON

Grand Central Publishing
Hachette Book Group
1290 Avenue of the Americas, New York, NY 10104
grandcentralpublishing.com
twitter.com/grandcentralpub

First edition: October 2019

Grand Central Publishing is a division of Hachette Book Group, Inc. The Grand Central Publishing name and logo is a trademark of Hachette Book Group, Inc.

The publisher is not responsible for websites (or their content) that are not owned by the publisher.

The Hachette Speakers Bureau provides a wide range of authors for speaking events. To find out more, go to www.hachettespeakersbureau.com or call (866) 376-6591.

Library of Congress Cataloging-in-Publication Data

Names: Stein, Joel, author.
Title: In defense of elitism : why I'm better than you and you're better than someone who didn't buy this book / Joel Stein.
Description: First edition. | New York : Grand Central Publishing, 2019
Identifiers: LCCN 2019009317 | ISBN 9781455591473 (hardcover) |
ISBN 9781478905967 (audio download) | ISBN 9781455591466 (ebook)
Subjects: LCSH: Conduct of life—Humor. | Elite (Social sciences)—Humor.
Classification: LCC PN6231.C6142 S745 2019 | DDC 818/.602—dc23
LC record available at https://lccn.loc.gov/2019009317

ISBNs: 978-1-4555-9147-3 (hardcover), 978-1-4555-9146-6 (ebook)

Printed in the United States of America

LSC-C

10 9 8 7 6 5 4 3 2 1

I dedicate this book to my brilliant, joyful son, Laszlo Stein;
my lovely, creative wife, Cassandra Barry;
my wise, generous father, Charlie Stein;
my insightful, warm mother, Rosalind Leszczuk;
and my honest, loyal sister, Lisa Stein-Browning.

I do this because displaying familial love might make you think I'm a decent human being while you're reading my horrifying thoughts. I also dedicate this book to political prisoners, sufferers of chronic diseases, and all the dogs in the world. This book is for you, even though you didn't ask for it or any book, since you're far more interested in freedom, a cure, and going for a walk, respectively.

Necesse est omnibus libris de commodis generis electi verbis Latinae linguae incipere.

It is imperative that a book about elitism begin with a quote in Latin.

—*Joel Stein*

Contents

In which our author recruits a person society has afforded no opportunities into the elite, partially by buying him a burrito. Okay, mostly the burrito.

In which our author creates a new, unbeatable party out of the elite left and elite right to save society, and spends far too much time coming up with a catchy slogan for it.

In which our author acknowledges that, as with all acknowledgments, there is no reason to read this one unless you believe you might be acknowledged.

IN
DEFENSE
OF
ELITISM

Introduction

I am carrying a bottle of 2012 Trump Winery Sparkling Blanc de Blancs. I received the bottle ironically, and I am regifting it even more ironically to liberal radio talk show host Stephanie Miller for the election party she's throwing four houses up from mine in the Hollywood Hills. We shall toast Donald Trump's concession speech with glasses of his own sorry attempt to mimic the elite he tried to bring down. It shall taste sweet. Slightly too sweet, due to the low acid levels in the Virginia grapes.

While Stephanie's guests chat and sip better wine than I brought, I nerd out on a couch with my computer, tracking county results. As I calculate the inevitability of Trump's victory, my vision narrows, and my blood pressure drops. It is awful to be the only person at a party who knows something, especially when it's that human existence is about to end.

I am not panicked because a Republican has won. Some of my best friends who own wineries are Republicans. Besides, I know Democrats lose half the time. But it had been 188 years since the elite lost the presidency, when the aristocratic founding fathers went down for good in the election between "John Quincy Adams who can write and Andrew Jackson who can fight." The results were not good for black people, Native Americans, the economy, or the smell of the White House, due to the enormous wheel of cheese Jackson stored in a closet.

The populist revolution succeeded tonight for the same reason it did nearly two centuries ago. The main reason Trump won wasn't economic anxiety. It wasn't sexism. It wasn't racism. It was that he was anti-elitist. Hillary Clinton represented Wall Street, academics, policy papers, Davos, international treaties, and people who think they're better than you. People like me. Trump represented something far more appealing, which is beating up people like me. A poll taken a month before the 2016 election showed that only 24 percent of voters disagreed with the statement "The real struggle for America is not between Democrats and Republicans but between mainstream America and the ruling political elites."

People are foolish to get rid of us. Elites are people who think; populists are people who believe. Elites defer to experts; populists listen to their own guts. Elites value cooperation; populists are tribal. Elites are masters at delayed gratification, long-range planning, and controlling our emotions. The most accurate way to determine if a child will be a member of the elite isn't an IQ test. It's the Stanford marshmallow experiment, in which you put a treat in front of a preschooler and tell her that if she doesn't eat it for fifteen minutes she'll get a second one as a reward. If she holds off for long enough, she might one day go to Stanford and create her own method of torturing children. Trump is a mouth stuffed full of marshmallows, little bits of white fluff flying out as he yells whatever occurs to him in the moment, which is usually a demand for more white things.

I started worrying about populism in 2008, when vice-presidential candidate Sarah Palin chastised the elitists, whom she defined as "people who think they're better than anyone else." Meanwhile, she thought she was so much better than anyone else that she could serve as backup leader of the world despite the fact that she believed that the political leader of the United Kingdom is the queen. After she lost she vowed, "I'm never going to pretend like I know more than the next person. I'm not going to pretend to be an elitist. In fact, I'm going to fight the elitist." She was unaware that there is a third option: to study so that you know more than the next person.

I became more worried two years later, when I was watching an episode of the *Today* show. Like all elites, I will claim that I saw the *Today* show accidentally, likely in a local NBC greenroom while waiting to pre-record a segment. Matt Lauer was interviewing Vice President Joe Biden about Elena Kagan's Supreme Court nomination:

> **MATT LAUER**   If she is confirmed, here's how the current bench will look. Five of the current justices will be graduates of Harvard Law School. Three will be graduates of Yale Law School, another will have gone to Yale Law School but graduated from Columbia. I have nothing against those fine institutions. I want smart people on the Supreme Court, but doesn't it sound a little elitist to you?

> **JOE BIDEN**   Well, I graduated from Syracuse University. Even though my son went to Yale Law School, yeah, it does. Your point is well made.

No, Matt Lauer's point wasn't well made, possibly because he was distracted by looking around the studio for an employee to sexually harass. Also, if I went to Syracuse I'd be furious that the most powerful alumnus in our history was changing our messaging from "Knowledge crowns those who seek her" to "We could not be more different from Harvard and Yale!"

A rigorous legal education is a prerequisite for a Supreme Court justice. Someone armed with only the common sense that Syracuse professors apparently don't ruin with book learnin' is going to have a tough time figuring out how Congress's right to "grant Letters of Marque and Reprisal" applies to cyberterrorism. Which it does. The last time someone made this inane argument that Supreme Court justices are over-educated was when Richard Nixon nominated G. Harrold Carswell—a man so dumb he apparently could not spell either of his own first names. Senator Roman Hruska defended Carswell's worthiness to be a Supreme Court justice by saying, "Even if he were mediocre, there are a lot of mediocre judges and people and lawyers. They are entitled to a little representation, aren't they?" Back then everyone mocked Hruska and didn't confirm Carswell. Now it feels like the opposite would happen.

We can't afford that. Populists believe our complex society is so secure that disaster is near impossible no matter who is in charge. Elites know it's not. Most of our work is calculating risk and planning for contingencies. We invented reinsurance, and if you give us a few years, we'll come up with rereinsurance. The myth that the elite are selfishly rigging the system while doing nothing useful conveniently ignores the fact that the system we've built is great. If this were a book about any other group of people besides the elite, this would be the part where I list all the amazing contributions we've made throughout history. I do not need to do that because elites created everything that ever existed except for Jell-O wrestling. The ancient Greeks came up with wrestling and university founder Peter Cooper got the patent for manufacturing gelatin, so the populists' only accomplishment is putting the two together.

When populists get rid of the elite, the results aren't pretty. In Cambodia in the 1970s, Pol Pot killed everyone who could read, wore glasses, spoke a foreign language, or was a doctor. Cambodia today is filled with some of the nicest, friendliest people on earth and has a thriving tourism industry. So that's not a great example. Still, you know how many Nobel Prize winners have come from Cambodia in the last forty years? Zero. Though I could see why you'd rather have nice people and tourism than a Nobel Prize, so again, bad example. Luckily there are plenty of other horrifying examples of the destructive power of populism: the Dark Ages, China's Cultural Revolution, North Korea, network television.

Populists choose incompetent leaders because their main criteria is whether they'd like to get a beer with that person. Elitists detest this idea, and only partly because we rarely drink beer, and when we do, we are less concerned about whom we drink it with than if it's made by a small craft brewer who was able to balance the malt with the International Bitterness Units. It's also irrelevant. Do you think Abraham Lincoln was fun to get a beer with? Our greatest president said drinking made him feel "flabby and undone," which is what your friend says right before you never take her anywhere ever again. The president who was the most fun to drink with was lifelong bachelor James Buchanan, who had a fauxhawk, was nearly expelled from college twice for partying, bought a ten-gallon cask of whiskey every Sunday, complained that the White House's champagne bottles were too small, and led us into the Civil War.

People's disdain for the elite has led us to downplay our importance, claiming, like Biden did, that we're all equal in every way. We learned this method of self-protection the hard way after being picked on in high school and beheaded in late-eighteenth-century France. It's why people who went to Harvard say that they "went to school in Boston" and people who went to Yale say they "didn't get into Harvard."

A *New Yorker* editor asked Andy Borowitz not to call Trump voters idiots in an article by explaining that "we don't want the *New Yorker* to appear elitist." Andy pointed out how that ship sailed in the magazine's first issue in 1925, when it chose a mascot with a top hat and monocle. Andy went to school in Boston.

We need to reappropriate the word *elite*. The only time *elite* is used positively is when it comes before *military*, *model*, or *athlete*. Even athletes aren't completely spared antielitist anger once they get too successful. Most Americans hate the Yankees, Duke basketball, and any other team that consistently achieves greatness. They think it's virtuous to root for underdogs, which is idiotic because preferring the worse team is valuing luck over talent and preparation. I am surprised people don't spend Sundays watching the National Slot Machine League.

Instead of fighting back, elites smugly quote Martin Luther King Jr., who rephrased these lines from minister Theodore Parker in 1850 about the evils of slavery:

> I do not pretend to understand the moral universe; the arc is a long one, my eye reaches but little ways; I cannot calculate the curve and complete the figure by the experience of sight; I can divine it by conscience. And from what I see I am sure it bends toward justice.

That's arguably true, but it's undeniable that the arc of a launched nuclear missile is short and bends toward the cities where most elites live.

We need to fix this while we still can, which is why I decided to become a full-time activist. Then I learned that being an activist pays even worse than being a writer. So instead I decided to find out who these people are who threw out the elite, what they want, and why—all of a sudden and all around the world—they have become so angry. I will bravely enter the centers of the populist revoltion, meet their leaders, and eat their fattening fried foods. Then I will analyze my data, reach conclusions, and issue a report suggesting we pretend to give these people what they want and do what's best instead.

This book is a call to arms for the elite. Not actual arms, since we don't think people should have those, but metaphoric arms, which are the type of arms that will be useless against the populists' arms, which are real arms. Which is why I am not standing up to the populists in person but here in print, where none of them will know about it.

I gather my lovely wife, Cassandra, and my seven-year-old son, Laszlo, and snake my way through the drunk, happy, clueless, soon-to-be-former elites at Stephanie's party. As I zombie toward the door, a woman sees my ashen face and asks if I really think Trump will win. I mumble, "I'm just a guy at a party," which she finds hilarious. But as of this moment, I know that's all I am.

At home, I force a smile as Laszlo gets into his pajamas. He's spent a year hearing every adult he knows demonize Trump, so I assure him that the election will not affect his future, which I believe insofar as he is seven and his definition of the future is one week. But I don't know what will happen after that. My stomach hurts. I know I will have to spend the next few days eating only bland, sweet foods, as if I had some kind of populist-induced disease that caused me to revert to their diet.

I fall asleep right after I say good night to Laszlo, exhausted by fear. At 3:00 a.m. Cassandra wakes me. "I don't know what's going on with New Zealand, but they're going to be full. I need other options," she says. It's hard to dismiss warnings from someone named Cassandra, but I tell her that the tricky thing about living through history is that you don't know which way it will go. Maybe populism will burn itself out like it did during McCarthyism. I add something about America's system of checks and balances, but she is not seven, and is disgusted by my forced optimism. "I need a plan, because you'd be one of those Jews who got on a train and said, 'Oh, fun! Camp!'" she yells.

She keeps naming countries we should move to, and I groggily spit out the names of rising far-right populist parties in each of them, some of which I may have gotten wrong, such as the Slovenian Justice League and Gunter Glieben Glauten Globen. As I do this, I think about the story Ronald Reagan told to the 1964 Republican convention:

> Two friends of mine were talking to a Cuban refugee, a businessman who had escaped from Castro. And in the midst of his story one of my friends turned to the other and said, "We don't know how lucky we are." And the Cuban stopped and said, "How lucky you are? I had someplace to escape to."

This is what I didn't know how to tell Cassandra: we Americans have nowhere to go. We have to save the elite.

PART I

The Populists

Of all dangers to a nation, as things exist in our day, there can be no greater one than having certain portions of the people set off from the rest by a line drawn—they not privileged as others, but degraded, humiliated, made of no account.

—*Walt Whitman,*
Democratic Vistas, *1871*

CHAPTER I

Flippin' Whippy

I am surprised by the sign proclaiming that I have landed at the Amarillo International Airport, considering it does not service flights farther than Las Vegas. People around these parts employ a literal interpretation of the Texas state slogan, "It's like a whole other country."

As I start my seventy-five-mile drive up Route 60, I turn on 101.9 FM, the Bull. Amarillo's New Hit Country is playing "Some Beach," in which Blake Shelton sings about driving down the highway in his truck when a "foreign car driving dude" on his cell phone gives him the middle finger. I nervously look down at the logo on my steering wheel. It's even worse than I feared. Why would the people at the Amarillo Avis curse me with me a Hyundai? Is this the "international" part of the airport experience? There's no more foreign-sounding vehicle than Hyundai except Le Car.

As I approach the town of Miami, Texas, I pass a huge wind farm. This seems out of place for one of the most conservative areas of the country unless they are gasoline-powered windmills designed to blow the smell of cow manure toward Austin. As the sky darkens into night, I turn off the empty two-lane highway into Miami. I pass the sole traffic light in town, which is permanently set to blinking red on two sides, making it an expensive stop sign. I drive over railroad tracks, past a herd of cows, and down a residential street toward a long, brown ranch house. A wrought-iron sign says COWBOYS AND ROSES B&B. There's a lasso over the word "Cowboys" and the word "Roses" is painted lipstick red. I park on the street, not sure if the owner or the other bed-and-breakfasters will need the driveway. I walk to the front porch, my heart beating harder than it should be for an adult male checking into a bed-and-breakfast.

Of the more than 3,100 counties in the United States, Roberts County had the highest percentage of Trump voters in 2016, at 95.3 percent. Located in the Texas panhandle, Roberts County is so rural it has more square miles than residents, and about 600 of the 925 residents live within the borders of Miami. I've come because, in the past, I've been found guilty of maligning people in print before meeting them, which taught me a valuable lesson: meet first; malign second. So I'm here, in person, to listen to real-life populists explain their political philosophy. After they ramble for a few minutes, I will teach them a little history, explain the fallacy of their arguments, and refuse their kind offer to become their leader. In the process, I'm certain to learn things from them, too. Not important things that will improve the world, but homey little sayings you can cross-stitch onto doilies and hang in your kitchen.

As with any diplomatic mission, I began by requesting an invitation from Miami's head of state, Mayor Chad Breeding. When I first called his office, his receptionist answered the phone by informing me that I'd reached "Miamuh," which made me sure I'd chosen the perfectly countrified place for my mission. As we talked, I noticed that she herself was not a person with a thick Southern accent mispronouncing "Miami" but a person correctly pronouncing the name of a town founded long ago by people with thick Southern accents who mispronounced "Miami." She told me that Mayor Breeding was traveling out of town for business, which seemed like an elitist thing to do, until I realized that he needed to leave town unless he wanted to do business with only 600 people. Mayor Breeding runs B&C Cattle Company, which breeds high-end Hereford cattle that are shown in contests and purchased in order to breed other cattle. I wondered if Miami is so backward that they give out last names based on occupation, like they did in the Middle Ages with Smith, Cooper, Mason, Baker, and Torturer.

A few weeks later, Mayor Breeding got back to me, offering to show me around town, saying it would be a "an eye opener," which didn't sound like a great tourism slogan. It's not as if there are posters proclaiming "Paris, the City of Eye Opening!" or "Florence: We'll make you confront reality!" He suggested I stay at a Holiday Inn Express twenty-five miles away in a town called Pampa, which made me think that the whole Texas Panhandle is a distorted version of Florida, possibly with a "Poorlando" and "We Don't Believe in Affirmative Jacksonville." But after searching around online, I booked a room at the Cowboys and Roses B&B right in Miami. I emailed Eva Creacy, the owner, telling her about this book and asking if she'd introduce me to people in town. Eva responded quickly, writing, "Happy to have him!" I explained that I am "him" and again asked if she'd be willing to facilitate some interviews for my work project. "No problem," she responded, followed by another message: "Are you coming to town on business?" I was wondering if six days were going to be enough to get anywhere with these people.

The month before I leave for my trip to Texas, several of my friends, most of my family, and my accountant repeat the same phrase: *Be careful.* My mom asks me to stay in contact while I'm in Miami and not tell anyone there that I'm Jewish, which seems tough, considering that I have to introduce myself as Joel Stein.

"Are you scared for your life?" asks my sister, Lisa, which is particularly worrisome since she is a divorce lawyer in New Jersey and therefore is familiar with dangerous people. She is particularly concerned that I'll enrage the locals with my elitism, which has long bothered her. "You have this belief that if someone has a certain type of job they're not worthy of your time," she says. I know exactly what kind of job she means: divorce lawyer. "If someone didn't go to one of fifteen colleges you deem acceptable, you think they're not in the same league."

"It's not called the Same League," I say, correcting her. "It's called the Ivy League." Though I also deem a dozen other schools acceptable, including Stanford, where I went to college, a fact that I have worked hard to hold off mentioning this long into the book. Lisa is right. As soon as I meet people, I try to figure out how to work in a question about where they went to college, often resorting to "Where did you go to college?" Assuming it is one of the twenty that it almost always is, I then search my memory for people I know from that school we might know in common. This means I care so deeply about where people went to college that I've memorized where everyone I know has gone. Meanwhile, I input the names of my friends' kids into my contact list because I cannot remember them. Which is particularly pathetic of me since they work so hard to pick memorable names, such as Jagger and Rocket.

My sister thinks the Texans will reject me after one look. "You wear tight pants and skinny jeans," she said. This is true. My two pairs of jeans are so uncomfortable I will only wear them for date nights with Cassandra, like my version of high heels. I did not want these jeans. If the Levi's salesperson in Manhattan's Meatpacking District had asked if I wanted hurty or not-hurty jeans, I would have definitely picked not-hurty. But the Levi's salesperson made it clear that the only way to get baggy jeans was to get a time machine, start a hip-hop career, or gain a lot of weight. I was definitely not packing those Levi's on my trip to Miami.

But my nondenim pants were also suspect. "You wear salmon-colored pants. Nobody here would wear them. All the men here wear cargo shorts," Lisa adds. I would love to wear cargo shorts all the time, though I would worry about not having things to put in all those pockets besides pens. What Lisa is not-so-subtly implying is that I'm not manly enough for Texas. Or the New Jersey suburbs. Being insufficiently masculine has long been an elitist tell. In the 1950s, the elite were called eggheads, a term first slung during the 1952 presidential election to emasculate Richard Nixon's opponent, the intellectual Adlai Stevenson II, who had a bald head shaped like an egg. Both Marvel and DC Comics created genius villains named Egghead, the latter of which was played by Vincent Price, who campily cackled puns such as "egg-zactly" and "egg-cellent." In Louis Bromfield's essay "The Triumph of the Egghead" he gave this definition:

> Egghead: A person of spurious intellectual pretensions, often a professor or the protégé of a professor. Fundamentally superficial. Over-emotional and feminine in reactions to any problem.

It's not merely my lack of masculinity, my clothes, and my obsession with résumés that worry my sister. My elite traits sprout from every pore, and the people of Miami are going to shun me for them. I have so many elite attributes that the most efficient way to list them is in a word cloud. Ironically, this is the least elite way to present information other than painting one letter on your stomach and standing in a line with other shirtless men with letters painted on their stomachs.

The greatest shame I feel in seeing this word cloud is that I only have silver status on United.

*   *   *

I regret my decision to come here. Mayor Breeding has texted me that he's going to be busier than he thought during my stay and won't be able to show me around. These people don't want me here. Nearly every person in every house as far as I can see voted for Trump. They hate the media. They want to drain the swamp. And I am a swamp monster.

Although every part of my body wants to get back in my car, drive to the airport, and fly to another country even though that would require a layover, I softly knock on the door of the Cowboys and Roses B&B, hoping no one answers. Less than five seconds later, Dee Ann Burkholder opens the door. She's a smiley grandmother with short blonde hair, funky blue eyeglasses, and three earrings, one of which is a large diamond stud on the top of her left earlobe. Dee Ann is white, as are all the people I will interview in Miami unless otherwise noted. There will be no noting.

Dee Ann waves me in, covers the microphone of her phone with her hand, and whispers that she's in the middle of a video conference call with fellow saleswomen from Rodan + Fields, the multilevel marketing cosmetics company everyone in the suburbs works at on the side, including my cousin. She asks if I know how to mute her conference call, immediately establishing our elite/anti-elite roles. I take her phone, swipe a few obvious buttons, and demonstrate that I do not know how to mute a conference call. Even though I signal with both of my hands not to, Dee Ann hangs up on her work call.

She offers me a seat on the red-and-blue-striped couch while she settles into a suede BarcaLounger in this museum of the 1950s, with its row of teapots, thick carpet, and TV that is not at all flat. Dee Ann is cheery, extroverted, and fast-talking, punctuating her sentences with either an explosive laugh or the approving phrase "flippin' whippy," which I eventually figure out means "fucking whippy." She takes care of the house for the owner, Eva, who works in Dallas as a nurse and has unorthodox investment strategies. When I tell her about my book about elitism, she promises to introduce me to all her friends the next day, relieving nearly all of my stress.

She makes me so comfortable that I slip in my first question about life in Miami that I figured I wouldn't ask for a couple of days. Dee Ann assures me that everyone in town has a gun, though she's not sure where hers is. Which is weird because her friends thought she was crazy for coming here at 9:00 p.m. to meet a strange man from California. He could be dangerous! Possibly a rapist! Or a terrorist! The idea that a terrorist would target Miami, Texas, suddenly seems as dubious as my mom's fear of my religious persecution. So, less than an hour after arriving in Miami, I reveal that I'm Jewish. Dee Ann laughs at my mom's concerns. It's like the scene from *E.T.* when Elliott and the alien see each other for the first time and both scream in fear, if a few minutes later Elliott tried to sell E.T. some cosmetics for his wife.

Dee Ann gives me a tour of the bed-and-breakfast, strongly suggesting I take the Cowboy Room instead of the Rose Room. As the brochure says, cowboys are "tough, honest and benevolent" while roses are "beauty, delicate and feminine" and have trouble discerning nouns from adjectives. There's a huge master bedroom where I assume Dee Ann will sleep, until she informs me that she is not staying here. Neither is anyone else, making the place less like a bed-and-breakfast than a rental house, turning this into a real bargain and an even less solid retirement plan for Eva. Dee Ann shows me the Keurig coffee machine and the stocked fridge, saying she'll be back in the morning to cook me my choice of a Wagon Boss, Cow Patties, Yellow Rose of Texas, or the Maiden's Prayer. I assure her that I can make my own breakfast and come up with my own ridiculous name for it. Before Dee Ann leaves to drive a few blocks to her own house, where she lives with her husband, Bill, a former reverend, I ask her for a key. Oh, she explains, we don't lock doors here in Miami. This confuses me. It seems like Miamuhians are skipping a lot of reasonable security steps and going straight to "gun."

After she leaves, I open the sliding glass doors in the kitchen and sit at the table in the large backyard and depressurize, looking past the mesa and up at the wide, star-filled sky. Dee Ann is more familiar than

I expected. She's not an opioid-addicted unemployed coal-worker mawmaw. She's got cool ear piercings. If the other townspeople are at all like her, I'll be able to persuade them to embrace immigration and trade and reschedule my return flight a couple of days early.

I wonder if the people I'll meet tomorrow will surprise me as much as Dee Ann did. What I don't consider is whether they'll convince me to rob a church.

CHAPTER 2

Baptist Row

D ee Ann begins our tour of Miami at the new $36 million K–12 school, which has 220 students. I'd assumed the town would have an anti-book-learnin' prejudice and reserve their limited tax money for police officers, police cars, and police action figures they'd distribute to children in lieu of books. But this school is a huge investment that will give the kids of Miami an amazing future, though not as good as handing them each $163,000. The school has a new rule requiring visitors to buzz in and sign a sheet in the office. Dee Ann thinks this protocol is ridiculous, whereas I think these are the types of reasonable steps between an unlocked door and a gun that Miami should employ everywhere. Dee Ann signs us in, without giving an explanation to anyone in the office as to why two people without kids enrolled in the school want to walk around the building.

The school is on Warrior Lane, a brand-new street, and the inside walls are decorated with the Warrior mascot: a Native American man's face with axes on both sides. Stanford refused to get rid of its Indian mascot until indignation at cheering for a stereotype of savage Native Americans grew so intense that it had to hastily pick a color for its team nickname and a tree for the mascot. This was in 1972.

We walk through the high-ceilinged lobby where kids are eating lunch at tables spaced out like a mall food court. Dee Ann introduces me to Lynn Lundberg, who is working the cafeteria cash register. When I tell Lynn I'm a reporter she replies, "People here are racist. I don't care what they tell you." This statement is not prompted by me asking, "Are people here racist no matter what they tell you?" I simply asked what Miami is like. If someone asked me what LA is like, I'd say, "The weather is great!" or "The ethnic food is really authentic!" not "People here are shallow, no matter what they tell you." Lynn says she adopted two mixed-race kids who are grown and won't even visit the town.

I don't know why I'm stunned. This is exactly what I expected to find. I have verified all my friends' elitist assumptions about rural America through my sharp investigative reporting skills, which consisted of walking up to a cafeteria worker and saying, "Hi, I'm a reporter." Still, I hadn't prepared to exorcise the town of its racism before curing it of its populism. The challenge before me was greater than the one Martin Luther King Jr. faced because there is nothing in Miami to boycott.

As we leave the cafeteria, Lynn stops us. I figure she's going to warn me of Miami's anti-Semitism. But instead Lynn informs me of something more frightening: Roberts is a dry county. Of the 254 counties in Texas, six have continued to ban alcohol after Prohibition, four of which are here in the Panhandle. As I'm trying to digest the fact that I'll have to get people to tell me why they hate me while we are all completely sober, Dee Ann introduces me to Carson Williams. Carson is a mustachioed maintenance guy whom people in town call "48." This is because Carson is always wearing a T-shirt celebrating Jimmie Johnson, who drives the number 48 Chevrolet Camaro on the NASCAR circuit. Carson lost his wife, also named DeAnn, a year ago, and lives alone in the house across the street from my B&B. He invites me to stop by any night for a "cold one." Roberts County, I'm later told, is the wettest dry county in Texas.

Carson and I both live on Lion Street, which is known as Snob Hill because of all the nice houses and residents flaunting their ostentatious collections of Jimmie Johnson T-shirts. Ada Street is called Baptist Row, home to lots of religious Southern Baptists. Down a bit from there is Criminal Flats, where people go to drink at night. This town has everything, assuming you only want three things.

Next, Dee Ann takes me to the Roberts County Museum, which is housed in an enormous, two-story, 130-year-old former train depot that sits on the once-non-ironically named Commercial Street. The only public places left in town are a café, a gas station, a convenience store, a courthouse, a bank, a public pool, and this museum. I am impressed they can fill a museum with artifacts from a café, a gas station, a convenience store, a courthouse, a bank, and a pool. Once we get inside, however, I discover that much of the museum is dedicated to quilting. The curator, Emma Bowers, is a thin, older woman with short brown hair who looks like she could be related to Trent Lott. She's energetic and caustic and fun to be around, putting her hand on my arm a lot while talking. She shows me a stack of classic Roberts County quilts, some a hundred years old, and I try to admire their quiltiness. "The new quilts go for pretty over comfort," Emma says disparagingly. To which Dee Ann adds, "It felt cozy to wrap up in the old quilts, but the new ones don't feel comfy to me." These people are so conservative that they object to quilting progress.

Miami is pronounced the way it is not due to a Texan accent, but because it was the home of the Myaamia people; the city in Florida is named after a separate, much smaller indigenous tribe called the Mayaimi. The history of Native Americans in this area is laid out in the museum's table-sized diorama of the Battle of Buffalo Wallow, which shows five white male dolls dabbed tastefully with bloodred paint lying on their stomachs in a pit, their feet nearly touching as they fan out in each direction pointing their rifles at the Native Americans. There's a painting next to the diorama depicting this same scene, which occurred five years before the founding of Miami, Texas. The plaque at the battlefield site, which is only twenty-five miles away, commemorates the one white man who was killed and five who survived the battle:

Here on September 12, 1874 two scouts
and four soldiers defeated 125 Kiowa
and Comanche Indians...
Stand silent. Heroes here have been
who cleared the way for other men

I now understand why everyone here has a gun. Otherwise, six guys could come into Miami, shoot all 600 people, and get celebrated in a sweet diorama. It also made me wonder why, given the massive military failure of those 125 locals against six invaders, this town chose to name its football team after Native American warriors.

I ask Emma if Comanches, or anyone else who is anti–mass murder, object to the town's celebration of the Battle of Buffalo Wallow. "We don't have any of that crap like in Charlottesville," Emma says. The crap she's referring to is not the white supremacists who marched two weeks earlier in Charlottesville, Virginia, but the liberals there who objected to a Robert E. Lee statue. There aren't any statues in Miami because public art projects are further down the list of town-planning priorities than doctor's office or supermarket. But Roberts County is named after former Texas governor Oran Milo Roberts, a Confederate hero who was president of the state's Secession Convention and a colonel in the rebel army. The stone marker planted on the courthouse lawn explains that the building is dedicated not only to Roberts but also as "a memorial to Texans who served the Confederacy." Like many Confederate memorials, this plaque was put up nearly a century after the Civil War, at the height of the civil rights movement, in 1963. That was the year Martin Luther King Jr. gave his "I Have a Dream" speech, Medgar Evers was assassinated, the Sixteenth Street Baptist Church was bombed, and President Kennedy sent the national guard to force the desegregation of the University of Alabama. If you were erecting Civil War tributes in 1963, it wasn't because you were a passionate US history buff torn between commissioning a statue of James Madison or Stonewall Jackson. Regarding the push to remove Confederate memorials like this, Emma says, "The world is falling apart. I'm glad I don't have any grandchildren." It's the same overwrought despair I hear when my liberal friends say Trump's election, global warming, or racism makes them not want to have kids. I intuit a deep lesson here about human beings: they are not nearly as fond of children as they claim.

Janie Gil, a ninety-four-year-old great-grandmother of twelve, walks in, clutching her quilting equipment in a purple velvet Chivas Regal pouch, which I fully believe she acquired before Roberts County went dry in 1920. Janie explains that she's a member of one of Miami's wealthy ranching families—the Gils, Lockes, O'Laughlins, Clarks, Paynes, and Hales. Their children sometimes marry each other, thereby concentrating their land wealth like European royalty once did. This seemed much more elitist than how people marry in Los Angeles, which is based on who is still available when your fertility is in steep decline.

Upstairs, they show me a Ford Model A, more quilts, and old photos of Miami. These pictures look like someone reversed the town's before and after photos. Miami once had two drugstores, two grocery stores, a hat shop, two doctors' offices, a hotel, and three gas stations. A bomb exploded here in slow motion. There's almost no one in Miami between eighteen and thirty years old. They moved for job opportunities.

Emma sends Dee Ann and me across the street to Miami's one restaurant, the Rafter B Café, which is co-owned by her son, Sam, the chef, and her daughter,

Susan, the waitress. Susan is harried, and Sam, who is six-one and heavyset, grumpily pokes his head out of the kitchen pass with a spatula in one hand to tell someone to "get the hell out" or yell "I'm an asshole!" It's as if he learned how to run a diner from watching sitcoms about diners. Sam had been accepted to the Culinary Institute of America in New York but didn't go, though his talent explains why my chicken fried steak with white gravy, biscuits, mashed potatoes, and onion rings is delicious.

Everyone at the Rafter B distrusts the mainstream media. After Trump's election, some seemingly friendly CNN reporters betrayed the townsfolk by airing a brief segment that focused on interviews with Miami's mechanic and market cashier. People in the restaurant are angry that focusing on those two citizens incorrectly implied that everyone in town is uneducated. I don't mention that that is pretty elitist of them. Still, if they feel this way, I would assume that they would make an effort to seem more sophisticated when talking to a reporter by, for instance, switching off *The Andy Griffith Show* on the restaurant television. Also, I would suspect they wouldn't talk to me. But these people can't contain their friendliness. As Dee Ann leads me from table to table, I learn there's a dog in Miami named Buddy that was trained to give a pained whimper at the word *Hillary*. And that most people here don't love Trump so much as they hate Democrats; religious Texas senator Ted Cruz won the primary here with 50 percent to Trump's 30 percent. This is a town so excited to be Christian that one of the residents is named Nikki Early Crismas.

After meeting 5 percent of the town, I finally sit down to eat when an older couple waves me to their table. Bill Philpott asks me what my book is about, and when I get two sentences in, he opens his wallet and hands me his business card. Charles William Philpott was a biology professor at Rice University, where he was the master of a dormitory. Loralee, his wife, grew up in New Orleans and has her doctorate in public health, specializing in neonatal care; she's also taught ballet. In his thirty-two years as a Rice professor, Bill focused his work on ecology and evolutionary biology. I do not know why they are here in Miami, but I am sure they are signaling that I should break them out.

I am wrong. Bill is deeply connected to the area. His great-grandfather pushed Texas to incorporate the nearby town of Panhandle, where Bill went to a high school with a graduating class of seven students. Bill had a friend mail him dirt when he was doing his postgraduate work at Harvard so he could sprinkle it under Loralee's hospital bed and claim his son was born on Panhandle soil. People here, he says, are different from the ones they lived with in Boston, New Orleans, and Houston. Bill tells me that when his dad's dementia made driving too dangerous, Bill disconnected the battery from his dad's car instead of taking the keys and hurting his father's pride. Problem was that someone was always coming by to fix his battery for free. This is not a problem in elite communities, where at the first sign of dementia we shove our parents into nursing homes and we have no idea how to connect a car battery. When I ask Bill if the people of Miami think he's a horrifying elite, he says that he keeps the details of his career to himself. Not because people would judge him for his eggheadedness, but because they would judge him for bragging.

As soon as I finish my chicken fried steak, Bill takes me two doors down to his office in the building on the corner, which must have once been a drugstore, a doctor's office, or a haberdashery. In addition to conducting academic research and tracking his investments, Bill paints abstract portraits, which are scattered everywhere. He's excited to tell me all about them, a professor in need of students, and I could listen to him lecture for hours, but Dee Ann has scheduled a full day of reporting for me and I've already fallen behind. I can't ditch my fast-paced elite lifestyle even in Miami.

Dee Ann drives us to her daily coffee group, which is being hosted today by Judy and Larry McReynolds, who live on Baptist Row. They welcome me in with a huge plastic cup of sweet tea, which is what everyone here is drinking. People in this part of the country don't have a lot of precision with language, whether it's "coffee group" or "international airport." I head into the dining room, which is decorated with more crosses than I've ever seen in one place, including churches. There are fifteen crosses in my direct eyesight. I try to remember if there's some holiday coming up that they're celebrating, like Cross Wednesday. But there's not. They love Jesus this much, every day. Larry is wearing a T-shirt that says UNKNOWN TO US, KNOWN TO HIM. If the fifteen crosses are a clue, I'm guessing the person the shirt is referring to is Jesus.

I ask about a cross sitting on a table that is so unusual it stands out even among fourteen other crosses. Larry brings me to the garage, where he uses a band saw to carve Reader's Digest Condensed Books into crosses before affixing a fabric flower to the cover of each one with a rope bow. I should feel badly that people in Miami are destroying books, but I'm relieved they're not burning them.

He sells the crosses for ten dollars, and I happily buy one, because when am I ever going to find a cross carved out of a Reader's Digest Condensed Book again? I tell him that I worked for Reader's Digest in the Manhattan office where they made those books, but Larry doesn't care. I worry it is rude to be excited about the raw materials of a cross, like bragging that you once worked in the lumberyard on Mount Zion where they got the wood for Jesus's crucifixion.

I join the McReynoldses and another couple in a game of Wahoo, a variation of the game Parcheesi invented in Appalachia. The two obviously appealing parts of Wahoo are that it's social and the board is shaped like a cross. As we move marbles around the board, it becomes clear that these nice people are sincerely interested in my life. When I tell them I have a son, my Wahoo teammate, Irene Edmiston, asks me, "Do you homeschool?" No one in my life has ever thrown out that question after I told them I have a child. Not only don't I homeschool Laszlo, I also don't home violin him, home sports him, or home math tutor him. I home make him breakfast and home read him a bedtime story, and I don't even do a great job at those.

As we Wahoo, my five new Baptist friends discuss an event that happened in Ada, Oklahoma—a town that happens to have the same name as this street, a German girl's name that means "of the elite," and was common in the 1880s when such sentiments were more popular. My lack of knowledge about current events in Ada, Oklahoma, shocks my fellow players. Bill Edmiston, a seventy-four-year-old housepainter with faded arm tattoos and a gray coif that could get a man elected to office in any state, shows me a Facebook Live video posted by the Gospel Station Network, a local radio station that seems to be the CNN of gospel news. Randall Christy, a Baptist pastor and founder of the Gospel Station Network, is reporting from East Central University, where Americans United for Separation of Church and State wants to remove the cross atop the Boswell chapel. "They're about to cut that cross off the top of that steeple! That's right. They're about to bring a crane in and literally cut it off," the pastor declares.

The video epitomizes the populist fear that colleges have ceased to be institutions where students acquire the vocational skills they need to succeed. Instead, colleges have morphed into brainwashing centers for the radical left. Only about half of Americans now think colleges do any good, and more than half of Republicans say they have a negative effect on society. This is crushing. Elites feel the same way about college as non-elites do about church. Actually, we feel even more strongly because we lived inside our church for four years and our church got us drunk and laid. And, unlike in real church, where they are smart enough to make everyone read aloud, we pretended that we read the boring books.

Education has always been considered elitist, partly because it was originally restricted to the aristocracy. America led the way in free education for the masses, but it wasn't embraced by all of the recipients. When most states made schooling compulsory at the end of the nineteenth century, many people resented the state taking control of their families. Billy Sunday was one of them. In the first two decades of the twentieth century, he became the most successful preacher in the history of the United States, traveling around the country to give sermons to audiences of more than

50,000. Once one of the fastest players in major league baseball, Sunday became the Elvis of Christianity, infuriating establishment preachers by running around the stage, sliding headfirst, smashing chairs, gyrating, and talking about sins in such detail that people would faint. One of those sins was going to college. Sunday preached that "thousands of college graduates are going as fast as they can straight to hell. If I had a million dollars I would give $999,999 to the church and $1 to education." This was a weird sentence for Sunday to put in the conditional tense because he had made more than a million dollars through his preaching. His appeal to lower emotions was criticized by educated preachers, whom he disdained for relying on history, philosophy, and, apparently, words. "What do I care if some puff-eyed, dainty little dibbly-dibbly preacher goes tibbly-tibbling around because I use plain Anglo-Saxon words?" he said.

The possibiltiy of a cross being chopped off a steeple in Oklahoma is not rattling me enough for my new friends' taste. To defend my sanguine demeanor, I toss off something about how East Central University is a public school and that the Constitution is clear about the separation of church and state. Bill says the Constitution doesn't say anything about a separation of church and state. I have been in rural Texas less than twenty-four hours, and already I'm getting ignorant conspiracy theories. I am about to argue with Bill when I realize how little I know about the Constitution. I assume the separation of church and state is in the First Amendment, or maybe a clause, or an article, or a section or a preamble. Possibly an amble. Bill says that the "separation of church and state" is merely a phrase Thomas Jefferson used in a letter expressing his fear of the pope suparseding the government, as had happened in parts of Europe.

I ask Bill and the rest of the Baptist Row gang if they think Christians are being discriminated against, and they give me a joint congregational "Yes!" that shakes those fifteen crosses. A 2017 survey by the Public Religion Research Institute found that 48 percent of Republicans thought there was "a lot of discrimination" against Christians, while only 27 percent of them thought there was "a lot of discrimination" against black people; 43 percent thought there was a lot of discrimination against whites.

As I move my marbles around the cross, I see it from their perspective. Even though they dominate American culture and politics, white Christians have been losing power since the end of the Civil War. There's been a particularly sharp decrease during my new friends' lifetime. In 1976, 81 percent of Americans were Christian whites; in 2017, only 43 percent were. There has been an increase not merely in diversity but also in meritocracy, which means that it's less likely your buddy can give you a job because he thinks you're a good guy. This has led not only to a more fair society, but one that is more productive. But as the

Commander explains to his female slave in Margaret Atwood's *The Handmaid's Tale* about the patriarchy he helped install, "Better never means better for everyone. It always means worse, for some." I understand that feeling. When I started my career, all the stuffy, white male editors in New York wanted my refreshing, narcissistic, sophomoric, self-assured voice. But now that women, minorities, trans, queer, immigrant voices are being heard, mine doesn't stand out as much and it's harder to get published.

Even within the confines of Miami, my Christian friends feel persecuted by elites. Teachers here are forced to tell their kids that the story of Genesis isn't true. Bill lists the attacks on their way of life: "Parents are raising their kids and they don't know if it's Johnny a boy or Johnny a girl. All these people wanting to use the bathroom and the lockers. Homosexual marriage in the churches." He informs me of a statistical oddity that he assures me is absolutely true: there are no homosexuals in Miami, Texas. He tells me this in a way that implies that everyone is homosexual in Los Angeles.

After Wahoo, the McReynoldses ask us all to stay for dinner. The only thing they're short on for hosting unexpected visitors is ice, so I volunteer to go to the town's convenience store before it closes. Larry says I don't need to. They'll go to the church and take their ice. I tell them that while I don't know nearly as much about the Ten Commandments as they do, I am sure "Thou shalt not steal" does not have the qualifier "unless it's from a church." They entice me into committing crime by telling me that the church has "Sonic ice." I do not know what that is. Is it ice shaped like little crosses? Ice made of holy water? Ice that makes a giant boom when you drop it in liquid? Sonic ice, they explain, is the soft, chewable, textured ice they serve at the fast-food chain Sonic. A congegrant bequeathed the First Baptist Church of Miami, Texas, a machine that makes such ice, and it's all ours if I'll shut up and get in the truck. I ask if, from a sinning standpoint, stealing is even worse when it's from a dead woman's donation to a church. They give me a look that says, "We all have guns."

Bill parks his pickup in the alley behind the church, partly for a quick getaway and mostly because it's near the ice machine. Larry has a key to the church, which he seems to think makes this all okay, but I think makes it more of a professional inside job. We take an enormous amount of ice and head home, the truck bed heavy with sin. Bill, oddly, thinks this is a good time to inform me that the rapture is coming soon. When I ask if he means "soon" in terms of biblical time, he tells me that signs indicate it will happen in his lifetime. Bill is seventy-four and has had heart problems. I'm not sure this ice will melt in his lifetime. I feel comfortable making that joke because Bill is definitely going to heaven.

When we sit down for dinner, I pile Fritos on top

of my chili and wait, not knowing when to start eating without alcohol to toast with. Luckily, Baptists have developed a workaround for the no-toast problem: grace. The people to my left and right hold out their hands, and I take them in mine. I haven't held an adult's hand besides my wife's in decades, and it feels uncomfortably intimate, like it did in junior high. Everyone bows their head, undoubtedly because making eye contact while holding hands would lead to making out. Bill says a prayer, which is not deeply inspiring. It's just a generic list of basics like "food" and "health." But I like it because it mentions me. This is the first time anyone has prayed for me in a non-mean way, and it feels great. After the prayer and going halfway to first base with these people, I feel closer to them than I did a few minutes ago.

The chili is terrific. As instructed, I mix peanut butter and Karo syrup together and spread it on my cornbread. It, too, is terrific. Then I scoop myself some more chili. And then some more chili. And then I have a whole lot of homemade apple pie. As I'm undoubtedly grossing out my new friends with the amount of food I'm eating, another couple stops by, uninvited. And then a fourth couple. Then someone's brother. And a niece. They say this happens all the time. The only way this could possibly happen at my house would be if we threw a party and put the wrong date on the invitation.

As the eleven of us sit in a huge circle on the

screened-in porch behind the house, I learn that these Trump voters are different than advertised. Almost everyone here either went to college or has kids who went to college; 33.2 percent of the people in Roberts County have at least a bachelor's degree, putting it in the top 5 percent for Texas. They're certainly not poor. Roberts County has a poverty rate of 1.5 percent; in the United States, 13.5 percent of people live in poverty; in Los Angeles, it's 20 percent. The median household income here is nearly 15 percent higher than the national average. Plus, $63,889 goes much farther in Miami, Texas, because there is nothing to buy here. They've even got a former billionaire in the county: T. Boone Pickens. ("Former" only because he's donated more than $700 million and been divorced four times.) Pickens owns a 68,000-acre vacation property with a 23,000-square-foot house where he's hosted George W. Bush, Dick Cheney, and Ted Turner.

The people on this back porch travel, and not only to Branson, though Judy and Larry McReynolds have been there fourteen times and the Christian-friendly version of Las Vegas is prominently featured in the T-shirt quilt she's making. Most of these people have been to California, and some have family there. Irene is from Verdun, France, where she and Bill visited this summer and stood beside the road cheering as the Tour de France rolled through. Jerry Wilmoth, a neighbor who has come by, usually goes with his wife to Manhattan around Christmas, and a couple of years ago they joined some other people in town on a missionary trip to Haiti after the earthquake there.

They're not as insulated as I assumed. I learn that the Hillary hater who taught his dog to whimper at her name had a beloved freshman college roommate from Saudi Arabia named Fawad, though he called him "Fuzz" and his prayer mat a "magic carpet." Bill's granddaughter is an atheist and her daughter also doesn't believe, despite all the Bible camps the great-granddaughter has attended while visiting Miami. Jerry's daughter is married to a black man, who he tells me is a great guy who fixed one of their trucks for free without being asked.

Convincing these people to trust the elites is going to be harder than I thought. They don't dislike us because they're poor and jealous. They don't dislike us because they don't understand our lifestyle, which they have seen not only in movies and television shows, but also in person. No, they gathered a lot of information, weighed the evidence, and then decided we were awful. And I am about to make it worse.

CHAPTER 3

Underthinking

J erry is a flooring-company owner with a beard, glasses, a baseball cap, and an ornery, Billy Bob Thornton demeanor. He squints, talks slowly, and tells a recurring, oddly dark joke about sneaking into neighbors' homes to take treats to feed his sugar addiction, which is a lot more badass when you remember that the neighbors all have weapons. Unlike everyone else on this porch, Jerry lacks an easy smile, glaring at me when I talk. He's the only person I've met in Miami who is even the slightest bit unfriendly to me.

As we sit on the porch not drinking, Jerry asks if I thought everyone in Miami would be racist. I pause for a while before answering, trying to figure out the nicest way to say yes. I eventually decide upon no, which is indeed nice, but doesn't get across the "yes" part. I say something about how I think racism isn't binary but a continuum and that I figured their views on race wouldn't be as progressive as those held by my friends. I become more certain that this is accurate when several of the people use the word *colored*.

Harold Stone, a handsome, bespectacled, gray-haired retired telephone systems installer with the vocal cadence of Mr. Rogers, tells me an odd story that several other people in the group corroborate:

One summer in the late 1960s a black family bought a house in town. They did this for a practical reason: they were hired as spies by the NAACP to see if the people of Miami were racist. The people of Miami discovered this secret mission because the real estate agent saw that the NAACP wrote the check for the family's down payment. By the end of the summer, before school started, the black family had sold their house, having determined that the people of Miami were fine, non-racist people.

I proffer a different interpretation of these events, one in which a black family bought a house with their own money, felt uncomfortable, and moved out. My story is not deemed believable. I will later email the NAACP to verify Harold's version of the story, and they will not respond because it is insane.

When Dee Ann explains that I'm a *Time* magazine reporter, Jerry says, "I know who he is." Then there's a long pause before he adds, "I've read your columns."

Humans generally add a compliment when they observe something about another human. For example, they usually say, "Nice shoes" instead of just "Shoes." After saying that he's read my columns, Jerry adds that he recently canceled his subscription to *Time* because it's too liberal.

Harold changes the topic to relieve the tension and prevent me from launching into a long-winded speech defending the fourth estate—which I'm glad about because whenever I finish that lecture, someone always asks what the other three estates are and I can never remember. Harold eases us into a less heated topic: presidential politics. My new friends offer facts about liberal elite politicians that I did not know. Obama, I am told, made beer inside the White House with taxpayer money. I thought home brewing would be viewed as a good, populist, American, Sam Adams–y activity, but these Baptists do not drink and feel that Obama set a bad example with his White House Honey Ale. Also, Hillary Clinton didn't talk about the greatness of the troops or the police enough. I am surprised to hear that the Clintons have killed people. Jerry says the media is purposely not comparing Trump to John F. Kennedy even though Trump was handling Kim Jong-un of North Korea with the same tough-talk strategy Kennedy used on Nikita Khrushchev during the Cuban Missile Crisis.

Two weeks earlier Trump warned that North Korea "will be met by fire and fury like the world has never seen." Jerry says that threat stopped Kim from launching any more test missiles. This seems like a weak argument because only two weeks have passed without testing. We wouldn't be able to prove causation over correlation at this point if Trump had warned Kim not to wash his bedsheets. To make his point clearer, Jerry tells me a story:

One of Jerry's flooring customers wasn't paying his bills. I thought for a moment that the customer in the story was going to be Donald Trump, but the allegory was less direct. Eventually one of Jerry's coworkers called the deadbeat and told him he kept a gun in his office and was an expert marksman. The check arrived shortly thereafter.

Though international diplomacy and quasi-legal debt-collection have many similarities, I did not believe this was one of them. Besides, this was not what Kennedy did during the Cuban Missile Crisis. During that horrifying event, American and Soviet diplomats negotiated with each other behind the scenes while their heads of state acted tough publicly to quell domestic objections to compromising with the enemy. Trump's public tough talk, on the other hand, helps Kim, who is dependent upon American threats of war to scare his oppressed citizens so much they're afraid to topple him and endanger the enormous military he leads.

After I spit all of this out, Jerry says, "Sometimes you can overthink."

"Sometimes you can underthink," I say in an elitist way I instantly regret. Yet not so much that I stop. I say that I don't care what either of us thinks. What matters is that the experts on North Korea, from the left and the right, thought Trump's belligerence was counterproductive. Jerry replies that the experts hadn't done much good in stopping North Korea for two decades, so maybe it is time to stop listening to them.

This is exactly what Trump argued. At a Wisconsin rally in April 2016, he said, "I've always wanted to say this: The experts are terrible....They say, 'Donald Trump needs a foreign policy adviser.' Supposing I didn't have one....Would it be worse than what we're doing now?" In a 2017 Freakonomics podcast interview, libertarian billionaire Charles Koch similarly said, "If you believe, as for example Hillary does, that those in power are so much smarter and have better information than those of us in the great unwashed out here have—that we're either too evil or too stupid to run our own lives, and those in power are much better—you have what Hayek called the fatal conceit and William Easterly called the tyranny of experts."

It's challenging to make an argument for homespun wisdom over educated expertise while speed-referencing economics professors, but Koch's point is that the elites always screw up. When Trump denigrated intelligence reports that Russia interfered in the 2016 presidential election, he cited that they couldn't be trusted because they were wrong about Iraq having weapons of mass destruction fourteen years earlier. Similarly, populists argue that banks can't be trusted because their mortgage derivatives collapsed in 2008. It's an argument that is tricky to refute unless you've ever dealt with a child. Their first method of challenging adults is to say that you were wrong this one time about that one obscure fact, so you're probably wrong about humans needing to go to sleep at night.

I call this reasoning error the Meteorologist Fallacy™. When the forecast calls for rain but it's sunny, some people conclude that weather reports are useless. This is dunderheaded thinking. Meteorologists know that predictions are imperfect. That's why they use those percentage symbols and try to distract you by giving themselves sexy names and dressing like they're going to a suburban hotel ballroom for a swinger party. On any given night, it looks like there's a 40 percent chance KTLA Los Angeles meteorologist Dallas Raines is going to deliver a televised marriage proposal to his tanning bed. Meteorologists are getting better at predictions, making the Meteorologist Fallacy™ even more ridiculous: three-day forecasts of high temperatures are now as accurate as one-day forecasts were in 2005, making a huge difference to people involved in aviation, commercial fishing, and last-minute three-day vacations. The Meteorologist Fallacy™ is used to dismiss scientists for doing their job, which is discovering new information by questioning previous assumptions. Sure, a few months ago a study said that chocolate was good for you and now another one says it isn't, but people who want to lose thirty pounds shouldn't base their diet on cutting-edge nutritional research. They should eat fruits and vegetables and stop thinking so much about chocolate.

Even when experts are wrong, it doesn't mean non-experts are right. A well-constructed experiment would compare how many screwups experts have made with how many non-experts would have made. While we can never know the counterfactual, we do know that expert economists bailed us out from a meltdown in 2008. Diplomatic experts have avoided a nuclear holocaust. Experts in statistics improved the method for evaluating professional baseball players, according to what I understood of *Moneyball*.

It's always been appealing to venerate common sense over expertise. In the 1920s Will Rogers mocked politicians by saying that "common sense ain't common." In his 1926 book, *The Klan's Fight for Americanism*, KKK imperial wizard Hiram W. Evans wrote:

The Klan does not believe that the fact that it is emotional and instinctive, rather than coldly intellectual, is a weakness. All action comes from emotion, rather than from ratiocination. Our emotions and the instincts on which they are based have been bred into us for thousands of years; far longer than reason has had a place in the human brain. They are the many-times distilled product of experience; they still operate much more surely and promptly than reason can. For centuries those who obeyed them have lived and carried on the race; those in whom they were weak, or who failed to obey, have died. They are the foundations of our American civilization, even more than our great historic documents; they can be trusted where the fine-haired reasoning of the denatured intellectuals cannot.

By exalting instinct over education our brains have atrophied over one hundred years to the point where we cannot believe racists used to argue against intellectualism by using the word *ratiocination*. In 2005, in his first episode of *The Colbert Report*, Stephen Colbert mocked this religion of instinct:

> Folks, we are a divided nation. Not between Democrats and Republicans or conservatives and liberals or tops and bottoms. No, we are divided between those who think with their head and those who know with their heart....Because that's where the truth comes from, ladies and gentlemen: the gut.

People are so eager to delegitimize expertise that they seize on predictions that turned out to be wrong, which is one of the two most likely outcomes of predictions. Failed predictions don't mean that experts are also incorrect about measurable data. Yet people such as conspiracy theorist Alex Jones love to conflate the two. "Climate change is real? Yeah, so was Hillary's lead!…They said Hillary was a lock. She lost. The experts are dead. No belief is certain. All is permitted. Go with your gut," he said. This is epistemological nihilism, which is a phrase you don't learn from your gut.

The gut is faulty exactly because it's inside of us. Common sense is individual sense, one tiny perspective, a single guess as to how many jelly beans are in the jar. As David Foster Wallace said in his 2005 commencement speech at Kenyon:

> A huge percentage of the stuff that I tend to be automatically certain of is, it turns out, totally wrong and deluded. Here's one example of the utter wrongness of something I tend to be automatically sure of: Everything in my own immediate experience supports my deep belief that I am the absolute center of the universe, the realest, most vivid and important person in existence.

Emotions are so unreliable that therapists heal people of post-traumatic stress disorder by telling them to ignore their strongest instincts. Not reacting to our gut instincts is why people meditate. It's the basis of cognitive behavioral therapy. Stanford neuroscientist David Eagleman scanned subjects' brains while they looked at photos of a needle pricking hands labeled with the names of different religions. People got way more upset when hands that belonged to their own religion were attacked. I got in the MRI machine, and his test revealed that I'm about average in racism. My job is not to act on those feelings. Our awful instincts are why the Ten Commandments are so important to these Baptists whose hands I apparently am itching to stab. Instinct leads us to lie, steal, cheat, covet, and ignore a phone call if it's from thy mother and thy father.

I do not say any of these things to Jerry. Partly because you don't want to push an argument too far with a vigilante who advocates death threats for late payments, but mostly because there's no way I could have thought of all this stuff on the spot. Also, the genteel Harold once again interrupts to break the tension, this time by inviting me to the Baptist gang's weekly Saturday breakfast at the Rafter B Café, which I happily accept. I like my new Baptist friends. They're smart, thoughtful, and, except for Jerry, friendly. I haven't felt this sense of summer slow since I was a kid on my own back porch, where my grandparents, uncle, aunt, and cousins would visit on weekends. Not one person here has once looked at their phone. They're happy to be with the same people every day. Elitists seek bursts of community at Burning Man, Davos, and a thousand other weekend conferences and clubs. These Baptists commune every night.

I wish Cassandra and Laszlo had come. He'd love it here, with the Ford Model A, the pasturing animals, and the unhurried pace. I tell myself that I'm giving him a better life with museums, concerts, ceramics classes, diversity, and a school carefully selected for his needs, but I'm pretty sure he'd prefer running around this town.

Without alcohol it is difficult to discern when a large gathering is ending. We are not about to run out of water, and no one is going to say anything so horrible they are forced to leave. So instead, a few people talk about being tired, and we disperse.

I drive a few blocks back to Snob Hill, double-checking the address before entering the Cowboys and Roses, nervous about setting off one of Miami's tricky unlocked door/loaded gun security systems. I pull out my laptop to go online to find out exactly where the "separation of church and state" is in the Constitution, and damn if Bill isn't technically correct, which is the elite reductive qualification for "correct." The phrase is not in the Constitution and exists, as Bill said, only in a letter President Thomas Jefferson wrote to a Baptist church in Danbury, Connecticut. The Baptists, ironically, were super into the separation of church and state back then, and worried that the competing Congregational church was going to become the official state religion of Connecticut.

I wasn't just a jerk about debating that point tonight. I was a jerk in lots of ways. Worse yet, I was smug, which is precisely what people accuse elitists of being. My dad always warned me of mistaking a lack of educational opportunity for a lack of intelligence, and that's exactly what I did. I chastise myself as I head to the Cowboy room, stepping over a small piece of rope on the thick carpet that some previous cowboy must have left while practicing lasso tricks. I sleep with the front door unlocked, which makes me feel safer than I do at home in Los Angeles, protected by bolts, a door chain, and an alarm system, each implying that I can't trust the people who live near me.

When I wake up the next morning, I see a text sent at 6:48 a.m. from Mayor Breeding inviting me to his ranch to "check some cows." It's stupid to turn down an invitation from the person I've had so much difficulty reaching, but it seems rudely elitist to bail on breakfast with my Baptist friends because a politician texted. Luckily, the mayor also invited me to the "33 Party" on Saturday night, an annual picnic celebrating the beginning of the NFL season. It's on the same night as the boxing match between Floyd Mayweather and Conor McGregor, which they're going to show on a huge TV outside. Like many events since the election, this fight has has become a proxy for Trump supporters versus Trump fearers. McGregor, a white star of mixed martial arts, which has a lot of white fans, is taking on Mayweather, a black star of boxing, which has a lot of black and Latino fans. Besides being a mini race war, the fight also has resonance for elitists: one of the most skilled boxers of all time is boxing someone without boxing experience. McGregor is a martial artist who believes that heart, instinct, and attitude count more than expertise. I do not know if there will be gambling at the party, but I am guessing I could get good odds if I take Mayweather.

My Baptist friends in the back dining room of the Rafter B act so happy to see me I mistakenly think we've spent at least one meal apart. When our food starts to arrive, we link hands, bow our heads, and Harold, the deacon at the church, leads us in grace. This time, I'm not mentioned in the prayer, which makes me feel great because it means I've already fit in, though it doesn't make me feel as great as being namechecked to God. After we eat, I take the check for my eggs and biscuit to the register, where Susan tells me that Harold and his wife D'Ann have already paid for me. I cannot believe how nice the people of Miami are and how many spellings there are for "Deeann."

Harold wants to take me to the only store in Miami, which is only open Saturday mornings, and not every Saturday. He calls the owner of The Whatever Store and announces that we're in luck. Despite its name, the store has a very specific theme: proprietor Rick Tennant only sells items owned by his father, who died four years ago and was a hoarder. Still, the "Whatever" descriptor is accurate. The store's wares include a container to keep waffles warm, eight-track tapes and VCR cassettes with labels reading "Quilting (only)" and "Quilting." I am tempted to buy "Quilting" to see what nonquilting footage it might contain, and whether it can be used to blackmail the entire town of Miami.

The Whatever Store has great prices despite its huge competitive advantage in being the only store in Miami, and both Harold and Larry buy some furniture. As I'm helping Harold load a table onto his flatbed truck, he asks, "Are you familiar with crafting?" I tell him that I am indeed familiar with the concept of making crafts, having spent my first year out of college in the employ of Martha Stewart, who remade frugal, do-it-yourself Americanism into an elite hobby. A few hours later, I drive to Harold's house on Baptist Row. As I'm parking on the street, I see Jerry and his wife sitting on their front porch in the house right next to Harold's, waving me over.

Jerry seems to have softened to me, so I don't mention that North Korea launched a test missile today, indicating that Trump's tough talk wasn't as effective as he thought. Instead, I take a tour of their gorgeous log cabin. They've got two cast-iron clawfoot tubs, a six-burner Viking stove, and a set of $1,200 copper pots that hang over their kitchen. They keep a thirty-two-foot RV, which has an electric fireplace inside it, inside their barn. They tell me that to supplement their flooring income, they own forty-three houses in the area, which they rent out. They are Panhandle tycoons.

They walk me next door, where Harold, D'Ann, and their daughter, Cheyenne, who has driven down from Oklahoma, are crafting in their gigantic shed. Harold reaches into a box and shows me something that shocks me more than anything I will see in Miami. More than the story about the family who were spies for the NAACP. More than the plaque celebrating the Confederacy. And I have no idea how to handle it.

CHAPTER 4

I Was Sent Here
by God

Harold pulls out a cross. One that has been carved by a band saw out of a Reader's Digest Condensed Book. A plastic flower is affixed to it with a rope bow. As I stand stunned and speechless, Harold asks me three questions: Am I religious? Would I like a cross that's been carved by a band saw from a Reader's Digest Condensed Book with a plastic flower affixed to it with a rope bow? Can he gift one to me?

I could lie to Harold, take his cross that's been carved by a band saw from a Reader's Digest Condensed Book with a plastic flower affixed to it with a rope bow, and never see him again. But I want to be as honest and straightforward with my new friends as they've been with me.

Before I reveal the awful truth, I ask Harold if I can ask him a question before answering his.

"How much do you sell your crosses for?" I ask.

"Fifteen dollars," he answers.

I take a deep breath, look Harold in the eye, and tell him that I already own a cross that's been carved by a band saw from a Reader's Digest Condensed Book with a plastic flower affixed to it with a rope bow. One that I bought from his neighbor and fellow servant of Christ, Larry McReynolds. Worse, I told him, Larry is undercutting him by five bucks.

To my great relief, Harold already knows about this. Larry had even asked to borrow Harold's cardboard patterns to use for his competing business, and he obliged. Harold has decided to turn the other cheek. "I'm not going to be miserable in this neighborhood over a technicality like this," he says. In Miami, intellectual property theft is a technicality. Almost all laws become technicalities when everyone has a gun.

In addition to the crosses—an idea popular among Christians that he first saw at a flea market—Harold carves the books into other shapes, which he thinks I'll like more than a cross since I already have one and don't believe that Jesus was the Messiah. He makes Cassandra a *C* and a tractor for Laszlo.

We leave the garage and head to their backyard patio when I notice Harold and D'Ann's car. It has a huge US POSTAL SERVICE sticker on each side of it. Impersonating the postal service seems a big criminal step up from stealing church ice. Harold explains that, even though they're retired, he and D'Ann are legally contracted to work for the US government, delivering mail early each morning to all the Miami residents. Harold also still works as a consultant, setting up the phone lines for a few oil businesses and T. Boone Pickens's estate. These Miamians are the kind of industrious, hardworking people conservatives claim to be. My job, in comparison, consists of hanging out with them.

Six more people come by, uninvited, and join us in a circle outside. Harold announces that he believes I was sent here for a reason, which doesn't seem like an impressive guess considering I told them I've come to report for this book. But Harold means that God, not a publishing contract, sent me here. Soon, all these nice people start to gently try to convince me to let Jesus into my heart. I find it flattering. Believing that someone you like is going to spend eternity suffering is the kind of major bummer that can spoil your buzz in heaven.

Jerry leans forward and tells me that Jesus saved him personally. It happened when he was a year older than I am now. Back then he was an alcoholic who had been divorced four times, T. Boone Pickens–style. Though he made more than $100,000 a year, he never was able to save any of it. He moved to Miami with $100 and a cardboard box full of clothes, drying out on his sister's back porch, directly across the street from here.

His drinking period is so foggy that not long ago he got a voice message from a lawyer looking for Patricia Stone. Jerry ignored it because he and his wife couldn't figure out who Patricia Stone was. His neighbor Harold Stone insisted he didn't have any relatives named Patricia. They couldn't think of any other Stones they'd met. Or any Patricias. The messages kept coming for three years, until Jerry remembered that Patricia was one of his ex-wives. Jerry had been to rehab three times and joined Alcoholics Anonymous, but none of it stuck. When he walked into the First Baptist Church of Miami, his body was physically gripped by the Holy Spirit and he hasn't had a drink since.

He wants me to read *The Case for Christ* because it was written by Lee Strobel, an atheist *Chicago Tribune* editor who decided to use his journalistic skills to find out if God exists. Even for a member of the media elite, this seemed a little cocky. But I wouldn't mind embracing Jesus as Lee Strobel did, since belief seems to make these people so happy. Despite what they think, though, believing in God is not something I can choose. It has to be part of your community the same way that Jerry's sobriety has been aided by living among nondrinkers in a dry town. Our communities control our lives far more than we do, and mine isn't religious. When Stanford students were asked to name their religion in 2019, 55.7 percent of them said they were atheist, agnostic, or spiritual.

My new Baptist friends try all the logical arguments on me, including Pascal's Wager, the risk analysis about how if God doesn't exist and you believe, you experience no big loss other than missing a few lap dances, but if he does exist and you don't believe, you're in for eternal pain, which is a big price to pay for a lap dance, which is already twenty bucks plus tip, and they keep the songs short. I explain that belief in God requires a Kierkegaardian leap of faith, and I lack the fear and trembling in my soul required for that dismissal of reason. After saying this, I instantly realize that another thing keeping me from being a good Christian is that I'm a pretentious boor. But I came here to see their worldview, so I ask if I can go to church with them on Sunday. They are thrilled and throw in Bible study on top of the service. I packed my Sunday best in hopes that this would happen.

I ask my new Baptist friends if they're coming to the 33 Party to watch the Mayweather-McGregor fight. They look at me kindly, like parents who have patiently explained how gravity works to a child who responds with, "I'm going to use gravity to help me fly!" No, they're not going to the 33 Party. They weren't invited, and if they had been, they would not attend. There will be drinkin', gamblin', cussin', and, depending how the night goes, covetin'. But they assure me that the people who are attending the 33 Party are nice and that I'll have a wonderful time getting to know them before we all meet again in hell.

Convincing these people to embrace a new political philosophy is going to be tougher than I thought because, in opposition to everything I've read about the fury of populists, they're happy. They aren't looking to buy into something new. They want to buy something to stop any more new. Even more challenging for me, they are concerned less about the rules of man than about the rules of God. I can be an okay debater, but not when I'm up against a 2,000-year-old book that is both the all-time best seller and infallible. I needed to talk to the secular thought leaders of Miami. Or the town's closest approximation. I needed to talk to the denizens of Criminal Flats.

CHAPTER 5

The Table of Knowledge

E arly every weekday morning, the large center table at the Rafter B transforms into the Table of Knowledge. That's what everyone in town calls the group of men who watch *Good Morning America* on the TV in the corner, drink coffee, and deliver unfiltered conservative opinions about international, national, state, and Miami news.

Other than Susan, the co-owner, the only server at the Rafter B is Vicki Ray, a skinny, long-haired woman with big glasses who looks as much like a sitcom diner waitress as Sam does a sitcom diner cook. Vicki, a struggling single mom whose deadbeat ex moved out of town, loves Miami. The residents helped her financially when she was in need. This is a town, she tells me, where the service station cleans everyone's car for free before a funeral. "You know the old saying, 'You need a village to raise a child?' It's really true," she says. I am surprised to hear someone in Miami quote the title and theme of a Hillary Clinton book. I am less surprised when, as soon as I mention this, Vicki tells me how much she detests Hillary Clinton. Then she tells me something that I had never considered: Barack Obama caused racial unrest. I figure she means that having a black president made white people uncomfortable, bringing racial discomfort to the fore. This is not what Vicki means. Vicki means that Obama riled people up with his racism. "Take the Trump rallies, for instance—Obama never said anything against it. It was implied it was okay. By a lack of action he okayed it," she says. It takes me a while to get out of my liberal paradigm enough to understand what she's saying. Vicki is arguing that the people protesting the Trump rallies were violent black racists, and Obama empowered them by not condemning them. "The black people are after the white people now. It's causing racism where there wasn't racism. It needs to stop."

Again, this sounds insane: I have strong evidence that white people are still after the black people. Klansmen marched in Charlottesville, Virginia, two weeks earlier. But I heard this same argument at that first dinner in town on Baptist Row. Several of the people sitting on the porch argued that identity politics divided our country. Instead of simply "Americans," people define themselves as hyphenates: African-American, Muslim-American, gay-American, Asian-American, Mexican-American, Native American–American. The phrase "hyphenated American" has been a complaint since the wave of immigration in the mid-nineteenth century, and it's used to scare citizens into fearing that the newcomers will betray their new nation, despite the fact that this never happens. Immigrants always integrate. Italian and Irish people, once considered so foreign, are now seen as indistinguishable members of the white majority. Yet this doesn't stop the race baiting. On October 12, 1915, as America was gearing up for World War I, former president Theodore Roosevelt gave a speech at Carnegie Hall warning against German-Americans who clung too closely to their heritage: "There is no such thing as a hyphenated American who is a good American. The only man who is a good American is the man who is an American and nothing else." Four years later, as the war was ending, Woodrow Wilson begged Americans to join the League of Nations by shielding himself with the assurance that he was no apologist for German-Americans: "Any man who carries a hyphen about with him carries a dagger that he is ready to plunge into the vitals of this Republic whenever he gets ready." A vitals-plunging dagger is a scary metaphor for a hyphen that merely implies you party on Cinco de Mayo, but it was not scary enough for John Wayne. In 1972, a year after telling *Playboy* magazine "I believe in white supremacy until the blacks are educated to a point of responsibility. I don't believe in giving authority and positions of leadership and judgment to irresponsible people," John Wayne released a spoken word album called *America, Why I Love Her*, which has a 4.8-star average in its 259 Amazon reviews. The album contains the poem "The Hyphen," in which he says that the hyphen in "Afro-American," "Mexican-American," "Italian-American," Irish-American," and "Jewish-American" fans the "flames of hatred faster than" the lines in a swastika. This is why "The Hyphen" is rarely played at bar mitzvahs.

After being in Miami for a couple of days, I can see that Vicki has a point. Elites may not have caused racism, but they've magnified racial tensions, in the same way that abolitionists exacerbated our nation's problem with slavery. Cops have been shooting black people for a long time, but Black Lives Matter brought attention to the issue. Fighting back does increase tension.

Vicki is upset that people like me in the media are taking sides in this tribal battle while claiming objectivity. "The media has been selecting who our president is going to be. They start telling people months and months ahead of time who is going to win just to keep you from voting," she says. This is wildly inaccurate. Members of the media don't care if people vote. We tell people who is going to win months ahead of time so we can get on television.

Susan walks over and quietly asks us to take our conversation to the back room. I figure we're upsetting customers with our heated political talk. Or that orders were getting cold in the kitchen while waiting for Vicki to deliver them. I let Vicki get back to work, and apologize to Susan. She tells me that she didn't ask us to stop talking because it was bothering the patrons. The only person the conversation was upsetting was her. "I can't stay in this town. It's been hard after the election," she says.

Susan is one of the thirty non-Trump voters in Roberts County. I am not outing her. Everyone in town knows. I should have, too, after seeing the cute, hand-painted rectangular sign near the cash register that displays a smiling, unintelligent-looking snowman and snowwoman couple that reads, SNOWFLAKE CAFÉ. ALL FLAKES WELCOME. I've met four of the twenty Hillary Clinton voters and one person who voted for libertarian candidate Gary Johnson. None seem as anti-Trump as Susan. She was a social worker in Amarillo before moving back to Miami to take care of a family member. She signed the lease for this restaurant so Sam could have a job. Now she can't afford to stop working here until the loan is paid off. She's so exhausted by the people of this town that she's not going to the 33 Party tonight and will watch the Mayweather-McGregor fight at a friend's bridal shower instead. In Los Angeles, bridal showers involve brunch, but I could see how a light-middleweight boxing theme could be fun, too.

Susan has never fit in. In high school she dated a half-black student in nearby Pampa partly to piss off her mom, Emma, the quilter who runs the museum across the street and is so upset about Confederate statues coming down that she's glad she doesn't have grandchildren. I asked Susan if she thinks people in Miami are racist. "I don't think it. I know it," she said. "They say things every morning that would get them hit anywhere else. Things about black people." She said during the Obama administration she heard her customers say, "Get that n——r out of the White House."

The Table of Knowledge is sparsely populated today. One of the few people here is the county judge. When I first heard of the existence of the county judge, I pictured a tough-talking old man in a cowboy hat who spits tobacco and wisdom in equal parts, hewing to a rough justice and possibly carrying stone tablets of the Ten Commandments, so also a strong guy. Instead, it's Rick Tennant, the proprietor of the Whatever Store.

Rick, a retired planner for British Petroleum, the same company his dad worked for, is calm, nonthreatening, and not all that old. In addition to the Whatever Store, he also runs the tire shop in the evenings, where people hang out and drink beer, serving as the informal bar of Miami. The judge, I am surprised to learn, lives in Criminal Flats. One of his favorite activities is coon hunting, which I am relieved to learn means shooting raccoons. He is sitting with a few older, silent men, who drink coffee and comment on the disastrous Houston flood without mentioning global warming. A few other comments about the news make it clear that the main difference between the people of Miami and me is that they believe there is only one right and one wrong and they're always right, whereas I believe that there is a shifting, multidimensional matrix between right and wrong and I'm always right.

Unfortunately, people at the table don't talk much. My presence has undoubtedly compromised the table's free flow of knowledge. Sensing my disappointment, Rick invites me to the courthouse, which has been restored to its 1913 Beaux Arts glory: high ceilings, carved woodwork, accordion-shaped cast-iron radiators. I meet the young county attorney, William Weiman, who is the only person I've met in Miami who wears a jacket and tie. He, too, returned here to take care of sick family members. Now that they're gone, he's not sure if he should stay. He hasn't been on a date in years. I suggest going on Tinder, but he tells me there are no local unmarried women his age. "I bet I'd have pretty lazy thumbs," he says. I do not think that is a sexy self-description for a Tinder profile.

The judge leads me to the cavernous, grand courtroom he presides in. If I were brought into this courtroom I would plead guilty to cut a deal, fearing that otherwise I'd be brought to the front yard for a hanging. Standing against the back of the room, I ask the judge what he thinks of elites. He tells me that

Washington politicians need to be term-limited because they get corrupt and lazy. He vows to serve only two terms as judge. I suggest that there's some advantage in having US senators and representatives gain deep expertise in specific policy areas. I figure I'll win this argument by making it personal: How long did it take him to figure out his job?

"Two years," the judge says, falling into my trap.

"If it took you two years to learn how to be a judge in Roberts County, it's got to take a long time to learn to be a US senator," I posit.

"I don't think so," the judge answers. "When you need help, you call the other senators."

I am considering arguing this point and asking him how that would work when all the senators would be relatively new, when I realize that, as a member of the elite, I can simply ask a US senator. I email Cory Booker, whom I know from college, and he writes back: "There are some senior senators I've come to really admire—on both sides of the aisle—whose years of experience have made them some of our nation's best experts on issues ranging from homeland security to child health care. They are invaluable folks in the Senate, who make a substantive difference on a host of non-glamorous issues that are yet still essential to all people."

I get why the judge and I have a fundamental disagreement about how complicated the world is. It's because we live in two different ones. In his world, you can rule on cases during the day, fix cars at night, and sell old VCR tapes on the weekend. In my world, I specialize in writing comedic first-person nonfiction prose and outsource my tax filing, gardening, housecleaning, job searching, salary negotiations, and — thanks to Google's Smart Reply feature — parent emailing.

But our worlds are more fundamentally different. While my friends spend their days putting thoughts on paper, the judge spent his pulling oil and gas from the ground. Some of his friends spend theirs raising cattle. If we were blasted back to 1900, they'd be fine. "Could you go a month without going to the grocery store to survive?" the judge asks. "People out here could." I cannot bring myself to tell the judge that I get my groceries delivered from Amazon Fresh. I could not survive a month if I had to *go* to the grocery store. What infuriates the judge and the people here is that while they're doing the dangerous work of extracting energy from the earth so I can sit at a desk and write, I blame their industry for global warming. And fly in two planes each way to tell them that.

I ask the judge what he thinks of my elite lifestyle, and he Socratically responds, "Would you leave your child with anyone in a ten-block radius of your house?" He isn't asking if I could find one person who could provide adequate child care who lives a half mile from my house, but whether I would let every single human being in my immediate area babysit. I live right next to Griffith Park. Some of the people living near my house are homeless. Some are professional musicians. I tell him that I most certainly would not. "We would. There's a lot to do with the word 'trust' here. We trusted CNN," he says. I hope I'm drawing a more complete picture of Miami than CNN did, but I worry that I'll fail because the lens I'm looking through is so different than the one used by the people who live here. My lens, for example, allows me to see more entries on a caregiver's résumé than "zip code."

When the judge pictures my life in Los Angeles through his lens, this is what he sees: "People are going to eatin' places every night. You're not having the one-on-one with your family. There's so much going on in the restaurant. Who's that? What's going on over there?" My family eats at home six nights a week, and when we do go out to restaurants everyone else is a blurry unindividuated mass. I would have a lot more trouble focusing on my family at the Rafter B Café, where I would already know more people than in any restaurant in Hollywood, where I've lived for twelve years. There's so little change here in Miami that the judge assumes that every new thing in LA commands my interest, including an unknown dining patron. I am accustomed to focusing through more background noise than he can imagine. I am shocked at how naïve he is until I remember that all my friends thought everyone in Miami beats up Jews.

The people in Miami are far more connected to each other than the people I live with. Most of them told me they were going to drive an hour each way to see the high-school football team's away game, even though the school plays six-man football, a version of the game originally developed for towns decimated by the Great Depression. I, meanwhile, don't know the name of my local LA high school. I can't leave my son with all my neighbors because my community is virtual. My friends appear on my phone far more often than on my doorstep. I don't know everyone who lives on my block by name. One of the first sets of questions on the government of Bhutan's Gross National Happiness questionnaire is a version of the one the judge asked. It reads, "How many people are so close to you that you can count on them if you: Are sick? Have financial problems? Have emotional problems? Have to attend to important personal events (childbirth, funeral, wedding, etc.)?" Cassandra and I, meanwhile, see a wedding invitation less as "an important personal event" and more as "an obligation to sit down together for a half hour and come up with an excuse for not going."

Nearly every day for years, I would drive by a window with a poster in it called "The Los Angeles Manifesto," created by two artists called CYRCLE. It had a white background and these words in gold:

We left our families
We abandoned our homes
We worked for nothing

We slept on floors
We partied hard
We lost our minds
We danced with the devil
We faced our fears
We swallowed our pride
We gave our hearts
We tried and failed
We followed our dreams
We are Los Angeles
We never die!

Judge Rick Tennant wouldn't see leaving your family and abandoning your home to follow your dreams as something to celebrate. He'd see it as the selfish act of a narcissist who deserted his community, history, and responsibility. I'm sure if I explained that I did it so I could party hard, lose my mind, and dance with the devil, he would be even less impressed. But the ideas on that poster weren't always elitist. Americans used to say "Go West, young man" instead of "Don't forget where you came from." Explorers were celebrated with statues, holidays, and dioramas in museums in Miami, Texas. Now half as many people migrate within our country as when I was a kid. Even when things are desperate, people won't venture far: less than a third as many unemployed men move across state lines than they did in the mid-1950s. Whether you stay in your town or move to a city defines your identity. White people who stayed in their hometown were 50 percent more likely to vote for Trump than whites who moved even two hours away. Populists are devoted to their soil. There's no way I would have done what Bill Philpott did and transfer earth from my hometown so my son could be born over New Jersey dirt. Largely because it would expose him to carcinogens. But also because I am not loyal to the tribe that raised me. I am loyal to the elites.

The people of Miami are attached to each other, but they are distanced from their country. They're living in a remote tribal island, untouched by the last thirty years. The rest of the country is Tindering and Ubering and vegan-ing and MeTooing and drag-queen competing. The judge found the little time he spent in cities to be uncomfortable. He cited Somali gangs in nearby Amarillo as reason enough not to go. "There's Vietnamese, Hispanic, African-American, and they fight among themselves. The Vietnamese will get in a fight with the Somalis. That's two cultures that don't get along. It's the same way in prison," he says. "You go to these countries and they don't think the same way. You have something they want and they take it. That's their culture." This seemed wrong because historically the culture of Vietnam has been a place where some other country sees something they want and invades it.

Miami, he explains, has to follow laws passed in Washington, DC, and Austin without considering how they'll affect rural communities. In that speech shown at the 1964 Republican convention, Ronald Reagan said:

This is the issue of this election: whether we believe in our capacity for self-government or whether we abandon the American revolution and confess that a little intellectual elite in a far-distant capitol can plan our lives for us better than we can plan them ourselves.

But as unfair as it is for the country to pass laws affecting the lives of people still living in the 1950s, it's dangerous for people in the 1950s to vote on how people in the twenty-first century should behave. Besides, these people are not Amish; the twenty-first century is part of their lives. If they want to use their smartphones to look at the Gospel Station Network and wear low-priced clothes from the Pampa Walmart twenty-five miles away, if they want to remain safe from North Korea's nuclear bombs and save their cattle from rising temperatures, then our country can no longer simply be run by people without expertise.

I'm not entirely sure the people here are even good at running Miami. This town once had a train station, two drugstores, two grocery stores, a hat shop, two doctors, and three filling stations. Children played team sports with the appropriate numbers of players. At one point it was so cocky about expansion it named its Baptist church the First Baptist Church. Miami had twice as many citizens in 1920; between 2010 and 2016 it shed more than 7 percent of its residents. Ever since oil and gas prices plummeted in 2014, lots of pumps have been turned off because it's not profitable to run them, which means people are working less, which means Roberts County's government took in $500 million in 2016, half of what it received the year before. Without a major upgrade, Miami's sewer system will break down soon. And while everyone says Miami is free of crime (the issue of the weekly *Miami Chief* I pick up lists in its sheriff's blotter "donkey out on Waters Street") and comprises no gay people, that's not true. And they know it. When I do a web search to check the spelling of the name of one of the nice people I met here, I learn that he's a registered sex offender, and his victim was a teenage boy. I like this town. But it has problems that the Table of Knowledge can't solve.

CHAPTER 6

Canadian Key Parties

I drive twenty-four miles to a grocery store in Canadian to buy a carton of Banana Pudding Blue Bell ice cream. I wanted to get wine, but I didn't have two hours to drive to get it. Plus, I'm slightly worried that if I brought alcohol back to Miami, I would get arrested and have to sit in the back of a police car for another two hours until we got to the nearest jail.

Jodye and Mark Tarpley, who live two doors down from the Cowboys and Roses, have invited me to dinner. I am more popular in Miami than I am in Los Angeles, which has 6,600 times more people and where I've lived 1,400 times as long. The Tarpleys are a smiley, ruddy, sweet, funny couple in their fifties who look like collectable porcelain figurines. Mark has slightly long blond hair, while Jodye keeps her dark hair short. When I walk into their house, I see that they are definitely Snob Hill people: there's a Keurig coffee machine both upstairs and downstairs, along with a wine fridge. Their living room has the largest TV I've seen, and it's curved, on purpose. Its cutting-edge, Ultra HD technology is being employed to show *Gunsmoke*.

Until the dawn of the age of Inconspicuous Consumption at the beginning of this century, belongings were a sign of wealth. Furniture and tools were so valuable they were handed down; I have the brass candlesticks my great-grandmother lugged all the way from Europe by boat. Now they could fetch sixty dollars on eBay. Globalism has reduced the value of goods so quickly that people have trouble processing this change, paying more for storage units than the value of the items they keep there. Elites understand this, which is why when you first walk into our houses, it takes a while to figure out if we just moved in or have lived there for twenty years. A *New Yorker* cartoon from 2015 shows a couple sitting on two chairs drinking wine in a huge empty space with the caption, "Only the rich can afford this much nothing." The elite's hero is Marie Kondo, who inspires people to throw everything away that doesn't spark joy, a rule I considered following until I realized it would mean always wearing a Bruce Springsteen shirt and no pants. Elites do not have second refrigerators or storage units. My TV is more than ten years old, and it is hidden upstairs so guests can't see it. Jeanne Arnold, a UCLA professor of archaeology who wrote the study *Life at Home in the Twenty-First Century*, noted how little clutter there was in my house other than books and wine bottles, calling our home "very French." The only compliment a member of the elite enjoys more than "very French" is *"très français."*

Amid their cool gadgets, the Tarpleys' living room is as cross filled as every other I've seen in Miami. One cross has a vertical bar made of the word *amazing* and a crossbar made of the word *grace*, with the middle *A*s of both words at its intersection. So I'm surprised to find out that the Tarpleys don't go to church. They don't even say grace before we eat some great cabbage with ground beef that Mark made. This is largely because they were brought up in different denominations they couldn't reconcile: Jodye grew up Pentecostal, where congregants spoke in tongues and rolled on the floor, whereas Mark grew up totally freaked out by people speaking in tongues and rolling on the floor. Even more surprising than not going to church, Jodye and Mark acknowledge the existence of sex. Jodye used to be a salesperson for Passion Parties, a company whose marketing strategy was to gather female friends, ply them with alcohol, and then sell them sex toys. "It paid for my mom's nursing home bill. She would have been mortified if she had known," Jodye says. Jodye once went to a sales call at a house in Lubbock, Texas, and discovered her customers were gay men. It was her most profitable night ever, and her most fun.

Mark and Jodye are both divorced. So is my bed-and-breakfast host, Dee Ann—and, recently, her son. As is Jerry. And his wife. And Mayor Breeding. More than three-quarters of the people in Miami I've talked to are divorced. This is not what I expected from a religious town. Especially one without new people arriving to have sex with. The Tarpleys tell me the divorce rate is even higher among the people they know in Canadian, a town north of here, where they used to live. They insist there were actual key parties there. This could not happen in Miami, where no one carries house keys. Couple swapping here would be more exciting, because they'd throw gun parties.

Jodye's divorce story isn't key-party fun. She says that her husband of four years was abusive and drank heavily. So she was not happy when Mark took to drinking in Criminal Flats every night on his way home from work, sometimes not arriving home until long past dinner. She'd lock him out of the house, forcing him to sleep in his car. "I have left him out in the middle of the yard in the winter," she says. Mark says that after three heart attacks and seven stents implanted in his coronary arteries, he has cut way back on drinking and stopped visiting Criminal Flats. Jodye tells him he has eight stents.

They've lived in Miami for sixteen years and love it.

When Mark caught West Nile virus, the town started up a collection for him. They say the people of Miami are trustworthy, unlike those on the coasts, especially the ones in the media. This is weird because I'm a person on the coast in the media who is taking notes for a book and they trusted me with some intimate stories. This is not the first time I've heard about the dishonesty of my profession and how, like lawyers, we use our fancy words to create loopholes to justify twisting the truth. The first thing Jimmy Stewart's character does after being sworn in as the Boy-Scout-leader-turned-corruption-fighting-senator in 1939's *Mr. Smith Goes to Washington* is walk into the National Press Club and go on a journalist punching spree. "Why don't you tell the people the truth for a change? People in this country pick up their paper and what do they read? It's not as much about being honest as being smart," Mr. Smith says before knocking a reporter to the floor. The camera then pans up from the fallen journalist to a portrait of George Washington, who risked life and reputation to secure the freedom of punching the press.

A few hours before dinner, I got an email from the Trump campaign with the same message about the media. The president made it seem as if elites were 125 Kiowa and Comanche surrounding his four brave white soldiers and two scouts. It read:

Friend,

The fake news keeps saying, "President Trump is isolated."

They say I'm isolated by lobbyists, corporations, grandstanding politicians, and Hollywood.

GOOD! I don't want them. All I ever want is the support and love from the AMERICAN PEOPLE who've been betrayed by a weak and self-serving political class.

Look—Hollywood and the media are going to hate us no matter what we say or do.

People here get this anti-elitism message all the time. The fact that they are so nice to me despite being told that I am their enemy says a lot about their character. But despite what Trump says, I don't hate the AMERICAN PEOPLE. I even feel like I'm AN AMERICAN PERSON.

As I scoop out a second helping of ground beef and cabbage, I ask the Tarpleys how else elites annoy them. Elites, Jodye says, lack respect for the law. Then she adds, "I don't have a problem with the blacks—"

These are the moments I hate most as a reporter. I wish I were indeed the manipulator of facts that Jodye thinks I am. If I were, I would give in to my instincts and stop Jodye midsentence, by spilling my iced tea or asking to swap spouses, which I'd have to do by tossing my car keys on the table since I have no house keys. I want to grab her and throw her in an MRI machine, not so she can see how racist her thoughts are but because no one can hear you in there. "I don't have a problem with the blacks" is the start of a sentence that has never ended with "but lighter-hued blouses work better with my complexion." And her sentence doesn't end that way.

"—as long as they're doing what they're supposed to be doing. Not selling drugs out here or having nineteen kids they don't take care of. That Black Lives Matter crap. I don't understand. If he had stopped and done what the cops said to do, you're not going to get your ass shot. I'm sorry. Then they want to have a big protest because Bubba didn't have his hands up."

This might sound racist. That's because it is racist. But, after meeting a local cop at the Rafter B Café, who knows everyone in town, I understand why people in Miami find it unlikely that cops would pull people over for no reason. It doesn't make sense. Which is the point Black Lives Matter is making. I want to explain that black people force their kids to watch YouTube videos of shootings over and over in hopes of figuring out how to follow police instructions flawlessly for fear of getting one movement wrong and getting killed for speeding. But I also know that cops are the personification of Miami. Being a police officer requires bravery, sacrifice, physicality, respect for order, clear definitions of right and wrong, and split-second decisions made from the gut. They have the last of the respected, well-paid blue-collar jobs. Insulting cops is a class insult. And while class insults are the point of this book, it is rude to make them in person.

As a person who has been scientifically assessed as a racist, I understand how a lack of understanding quickly devolves into tribalism. I have been following news about the upcoming Mayweather–McGregor fight so I don't seem too unmanly at the party. I read a column by Bryan Armen Graham, the deputy sports editor of the *Guardian*, who said that "the Mayweather-McGregor farce is the event our Idiocracy deserves," arguing that there's no way McGregor "can catch up to the fistic aptitude of Mayweather, who's been drilled in the mysteries of the sport since childhood. There's no such thing as a crash course for a lifelong craft." Graham predicted that without a close contest to hype, the fight promotion would degrade to race baiting. He was right. McGregor, who is from Ireland, is so Irish he went to a Gaelcholáiste called Coláiste de hÍde in Tallaght. That could be a pub and it would still be the most Irish-sounding thing in the world, but it's the one thing even more Irish than a drinking establishment: it's a Gaelic-language-immersion high school. When reporters accused him of racism for calling Mayweather "boy" and referring to *Rocky III* as the movie "with the dancing monkeys," McGregor apologized by saying, "A lot of media seem to be saying I'm against black people. That's absolutely fucking ridiculous. Do they not know I'm half black? Yeah. I'm half black from the belly button down." This does not sound any less offensive in Gaelic.

Before I leave, the Tarpleys invite my family and me to visit Miami and stay at their house. I got the same invitation from Harold and D'Ann. And Jerry and his wife. It's incredibly generous, all these meals and invitations. I finally know what people mean when they come back from distant lands talking about how friendly the locals are.

Jerry told me that he and his wife are coming to Los Angeles next summer. As soon as he said it, I worried that if he called me, I wouldn't invite him to stay in my house. I called Cassandra to test how she'd feel about my new Miami friends staying with us, and she said what I feared I, too, felt: she'd rather not. She reassures me it is not because we are bad people. She grew up in Hoosick Falls, New York, a town that is nearly as tiny but way less friendly than Miami, and even though she's an introvert she would get excited when anyone visited. She explains that I'm serving as entertainment in a place that never gets visitors, whereas in Los Angeles, we are so overloaded with social obligations that the default reaction is to fend people off.

But I wondered if there is a darker reason that I wouldn't be eager to put my new Baptist friends up when they're in Los Angeles. If I was at the Nobel Banquet and some laureates told me they were coming to LA, I think I'd invite them to stay a whole week. I may like the people of Miami, but I fear that the elitist in me doesn't. I don't like the idea that I might be like that. I feel morally inferior to the people of Miami.

Then I have an even darker thought: if, instead of being a *Time* magazine columnist, I were another roustabout working the rigs for a week, would these people invite me to come back and stay at their houses? Is it possible that Jerry, who had read my columns, didn't grow to like me over the last two days, but was negging me at first to try to make me want to win him over, like a pickup artist does with a woman at a bar? Is it possible that networking and social ladder climbing aren't noxious by-products of the elite but of all humanity? I hope none of that is true and that I am projecting the worst of me onto the best of Miami.

I walk to the Cowboys and Roses, open my door, and head to the Cowboy bedroom, once again passing that small piece of rope on the carpet. Instead of stepping over it, I kick it out of the way with my bare toe. At which point the rope moves. I look closely, run away, go to the Internet, come back, look at a greater distance, and confirm it is not a Texan Moving Rope. It is a tiny scorpion.

I start to feel a warm throbbing in my foot that is definitely psychosomatic and definitely going to get worse. I grab a huge Time-Life book about the Old West, and, instead of looking up how to suck scorpion venom from a toe, slam it on top of the scorpion, which hasn't moved despite all the loud, screechy noises I've been making. I peel the book off, vacuum the flattened scorpion remains, head to my room, and start the real work of panicking.

The "How Do You Handle a Scorpion Sting?" entry on WebMD starts a little cutesy for my current tastes: "A jab from this critter's curvy tail is painful, but it rarely causes an allergic reaction." I'm greatly relieved. But then, in paragraph three, WebMD's tone changes dramatically: "It might be a different story if you live in the US Southwest." Which is where I am. That's a massive group of people to initially reassure with those first two paragraphs. Stings from scorpions in the Southwest can cause a racing heart, weakness, and muscle twitches, all of which I now feel. Victims should go to an emergency room for antivenom. Luckily, the dangerous scorpions are black scorpions, and mine is tan. I am feeling much calmer until I read that sentence a fifth time and realize that the dangerous Southwest species aren't "black scorpions" but "bark scorpions," which are tan colored. Just call them tan scorpions. There's no need to be clever when naming venomous animals. I am now furious at both WebMD and arachnologists. I search for broken skin on my toe, but I haven't looked at my toe in years and can't remember what it's supposed to look like. As I'm inspecting my toe, I see a far larger scorpion on the floor on top of a pair of my shorts. I grab a corner of my shorts to fling it off, but before I can, it scampers into the pocket. I open the unlocked front door and fling my shorts as far as I can into the middle of the front yard.

I decide not to drive to the hospital, since it's twenty-five miles away and, undoubtedly, full of people who got accidentally shot while stopping by a neighbor's house. I get in bed gingerly, covering myself tightly in the top sheet. I plan to go to a hardware store tomorrow to buy a black light to search the house for more scorpions. Then I remember there are no hardware stores here.

Early the next morning I walk into the yard to retrieve my shorts before anyone on Snob Hill notices. I shake them out, to be safe, and the giant scorpion pops out of the pocket it crawled into last night. Apparently scorpions like to stay in the dark and not explore much outside of their tiny area. They are a very cheap metaphor for Miami, Texas, that I have decided not to use, not because I've become nicer, but because there's a more obvious metaphor for my barefooted scorpion interaction. One that says my mission to convert the populists is worthy. That I should not give up.

In the Gospel of Luke, Jesus sends out seventy disciples as missionaries, telling them to enter strangers' houses barefoot, eating and drinking whatever they're offered because their work is worthy. He then says to his sandal-less disciples, "I give to you the authority to tread upon serpents and scorpions, and on all the power of the enemy, and nothing by any means shall hurt you; but, in this rejoice not that the spirits are subjected to you, but rejoice rather that your names were written in the heavens." I have tread upon scorpions and nothing hurt me. I also, in case Eva Creacy brings it up, had authority via Luke 10:7 to eat and drink whatever is offered, including all those coffee pods missing from next to the Keurig machine.

I shall rejoice and continue my mission. Unless I die from bark scorpion venom.

CHAPTER 7

An Unclean Spirit

I enter the nave of the First Baptist Church in my khakis and button-up shirt, and am immediately approached by a cheery, short, curly-haired older man in short-sleeves. He informs me of two things, one without even speaking: he is the pastor and I have overdressed. I start to introduce myself but he tells me he already knows all about me and leads me to Jerry's bible study group. I pretend not to know my way around, lest I tip him off about the Great Sonic Ice Heist.

There are a dozen adults of various ages and genders but not races seated around a table in a small conference room. Jerry sits at the head, wearing a white button-down shirt and no baseball cap, looking like Tom Sawyer bathed by his aunt for church. I am welcomed to the room with a verse from Hebrews 13:2 written on the wall: "Be not forgetful to entertain strangers. For some have entertained angels unaware." Though I like this line a lot, I don't understand it. We should only be nice to people because they might have hung out with angels? How great can these people be if angels were sent to spy on them? What kind of idiot has an angel over for dinner and doesn't notice the wings and halo? What types of entertainment do angels prefer? Should you put on Handel's Concerto in B-Flat Major for Harp or would that be racist? We hadn't even started Bible study and I already had a lot of questions.

Though I've never been to a Bible study, I have a clear picture of how it will work, based on studying other books. I figure we'll take a section, analyze the text, and try to discern the meaning by bringing in historical context, authorial intent, reader-response theory, close reading, and deconstructionism. This is not what happens. Instead, we take out our books, which, to my surprise, are not Bibles. They are more like magazines, called *Adults' Bible Study for Life*, Summer 2017. We turn to today's entry on page 123, which asks us to discuss two sentences, Mark 5:1–2.

They came to the other side of the sea, to the country of the Gerasenes. And when Jesus had stepped out of the boat, immediately there met him out of the tombs a man with an unclean spirit.

As per the magazine's instruction, Jerry talks about how we can be nicer to people in need. Not long ago, he saw a homeless guy in San Francisco and wondered what to do. "Do you shy away from it? Do you turn to the government? Or do you handle it?" he asks.

Do I "handle it"? How am I supposed to "handle it"? Invite the screaming methed-out schizophrenic guy to live with my family even though none of us has experience handling mental illness or drug addiction and one of us is eight years old? Of course I let the government handle it. I also let the government handle it when I see a pothole or an invading foreign army.

Other people start talking about even more tangentially related stuff in their own lives, and I begin to realize Bible study is like any other book club, except without wine. Ignoring the reading seems even worse here than in a book club, since the author is God and therefore knows we're ignoring His work. To get us back to the text, I ask for context for the two biblical sentences we're supposed to be studying. Harold explains they're part of the story in which Jesus performed an exorcism on a possessed man. It turned out this guy had a lot of demons, who collectively called themselves Legion. To spare the demons the fate of returning to hell, he threw their spirits into a herd of 2,000 pigs, which then drowned themselves in a lake. There seems to me like a lot to unpack here before we discuss how to help the homeless. Questions such as: Who had a herd of thousands of pigs in the pre–factory farming era? How do we reconcile what Jesus did through the lens of animal rights? Or the rights of villagers whose property values plummeted after the town's beautiful pond was polluted by 2,000 rotting demon pigs?

Instead of exploring any of this, Jerry says that Jesus ridding the possessed man of demon spirits makes him realize that people can get along if they simply talk. Like he has with me. Jerry says that maybe instead of having a US Senate, we should get people from all over the country to meet and work out our problems. This suggestion makes me insane, since that's precisely what the US Senate is. I think he means that senators should be people like Jerry and me, instead of professionals. Which makes me more insane.

After ending Bible study by, yet again, holding hands and praying, we go to the nave for a service that is based on the ancient tradition of television shows. There are three screens behind the altar that flash segues to the segments in today's episode. During "Children's Sermon," six kids sit onstage while the pastor makes paper hats, which represent the wonder of faith, and gives them lollipops, which represent lollipops. We end with prayers, in which about a third of the forty people in the congregation bare personal traumas. One has a sister in Houston whose house is flooded. Another has a spouse in the hospital with late-stage cancer. We had prayed for each other in the same way at the end of Bible study, our heads bowed as people bared their pain. I had assumed people were exposing their grief to get more voices to petition God, as if the increased volume would up their chances. But that's not the main reason. This is a rare opportunity to be heard without any reaction—no risk of interruption, judgment, or not seeing the exact empathy you need in the listener's eyes. More importantly, you're empowering the community to comfort you without having to ask. I do not feel the spirit of Jesus, but for one of the first times in my life, I feel the spirit of populism. When the screen displays "Tithes and Offering," I pull out a five-dollar bill, but Dee Ann yanks the plate away before I can drop it in. As nice as that is of her, I wish she hadn't.

After the service, I follow my Baptist crew as we drive a few blocks to Dee Ann's house, where she's laid out an amazing spread: ribs, scalloped potatoes, green beans, roasted potatoes, banana pudding. The men are served first and sit at the dining room table while the women eat in the den. This seems strange, since they should be with us, performing dances and massaging our feet. We men hold hands and bow our heads while Dee Ann's husband, Bill, leads us in a thoughtful prayer. Bill is a tall, shiny-headed, football-wide former preacher, who retired in 2004 after forty-two years working in churches. He speaks slowly, but animatedly, having kept the fervent excitement of learning he first had as a farm boy who earned a college scholarship. More professor than proselyltzer, he has a breadth and depth of knowledge that exceeds Bill Philpott's. Thanks to a stint working with the Jewish community in Kansas City, he teaches me more Yiddish words than my grandmothers did. The people of Miami respect him so greatly that even though he moved here only two years ago and has never preached in town, one fellow congregant casually asked him which bank held his mortgage and then, to Bill and Dee Ann's surprise, paid off their loan.

I'm deep into my third helping of banana pudding when Harold tells me a story I've already heard from others in town. It takes place years ago, at Miami's biggest event, the annual Cow Calling Championship. A cranky old man from town marched down the middle of the parade wearing a KKK hood. It was particularly upsetting because there was a local black family there, this one also undoubtedly spying for the NAACP. The point of the story is that everyone in town felt awful and embarrassed about the incident because they're good people. Which is not the moral I take away, which is that Miami is a town where you can wear a KKK hood in a parade and not get the crap beaten out of you.

I leave Dee Ann and Bill's house full and happy, though a bit like a plushkin who schwindleraied the goyim with my naarishkeit. I head back to the Cowboys and Roses, check for scorpions, and wonder if I'll see my Baptist friends again.

My wondering does not last long. I've barely put

a coffee pod into the Keurig machine when I get an email from Zachary McDowell. He and his wife, Pamela, were the only people younger than me at Bible study. He has a long hipster beard and she was wearing a tight, brightly patterned, stylish dress with a dramatic diagonal hem. They were the first people I saw in Miami who looked like they could be my neighbors in Los Angeles. The McDowells have a six-year-old son named Rifle. I assumed he was the only person named Rifle in America, but he was not even the only person named Rifle in Miami, Texas. Zachary got the idea for the name after meeting the town's adult Rifle. "I like guns and I like hunting. It sort of represents what we do. And in a pregnant delusional state she agreed," Zachary said as Pamela nodded. "And Remington was becoming too popular." They named their daughter Veronica Lake McDowell. One thing the elite and populists have is in common is spending way much time thinking of weird names for their kids.

Zachary has long wondered what the Cowboys and Roses looks like, so I give him a tour. After, he offers to take me on a drive. Without locking up, I go outside, where I see his GMC Sierra three-quarter-ton diesel pickup truck. Its engine is running. Which means it's been running for the last fifteen minutes. I feel awful, but Zachary can't figure out what the big deal is. Would something happen to my truck if I left it on outside my house in Los Angeles? Yes, I tell him, definitely. If I left my convertible yellow Mini Cooper running for fifteen minutes on the street, it would either be stolen or surrounded by protestors from the National Resources Defense Council.

We drive out of Miami onto Route 60 and I ask Zachary where we're going, hoping it's a coffee shop or a restaurant. He tells me that people here like to drive around. Like to nowhere. As a form of entertainment. This is insane. Being stuck in a car is the main thing everyone in my city complains about. I wonder what else Angelenos hate that these people would love. So far, I know the list includes driving, carbs, and tourists.

We pass a truck pulled over on the empty highway and Zachary stops to see what's wrong. Luckily, everything is fine and we wave a lot as we drive away. "Around here everybody waves," he says. That's one of the things he didn't like when he moved to Denver for a short time. "In that big city everyone is in their bubble. I felt like, 'Why is that guy not saying hello?' When you grow up a country boy it feels uncomfortable." I've never been a country boy but I've always felt the same way. Living in a city is like constantly being on an airplane, pretending people right next to us don't exist. The judge was right: it's weird that I ignore the people sitting near me at an eatin' place. It's weird that I don't know all the people living within a half mile of my house. It's weird that the people in Los Angeles don't wave when we see each other.

White people only feel secure enough to wave when engaging in activities in which we're nearly certain everyone else will be white, such as hiking, boating, driving a golf cart, riding a motorcycle, and being Queen of England. Though it might simply be that Angelenos don't have the arm strength to wave 4 million times a day.

Zachary doesn't like going to cities now, including Amarillo. A couple of weeks ago, his car was broken into while he was at a rock concert there. He says he felt violated, but was fortunate that they didn't take anything valuable, just some change and an inexpensive gun he kept in his car. Having a gun stolen by criminals seems less like an epilogue and more like the way I would start a story. But Zachary's fear of Amarillo has less to do with criminals he has unwittingly armed than with undocumented immigrants. "Every time you hear about a crime on 710 AM, it's a Latin last name," he says.

We park at a huge canyon so Zachary can show me what he does for a living. He pours fetid bacteria into a fire hydrant–sized natural gas wellhead so it can clean the pipes by eating the gunk. Though it's stored tightly in canisters, it smells up the back of his truck no matter how much he cleans it. This is not what he expected to be doing after he studied golf course and landscape technology in college. But he couldn't stand the snobs at the Denver country club, so he moved back here. Still, I can see that Denver is still in him. He's wearing a fifty-dollar Irish flat cap from the Goorin Bros, which has a store two miles from my house that is so intimidatingly trendy I've never entered it. He does CrossFit workouts in Pampa. He drinks matcha tea for the antioxidants. He likes the same standup comedians I do. He still talks regularly to one of his best friends in Colorado, a seventy-year-old gay man. What Zachary learned from that relationship wasn't that gay marriage should be legal, but that while homosexual sex is a sin, all of us struggle with sin and we should refrain from judging others.

We're ninety miles out of Miami. I like Zachary a lot, but I love my wife way more, and if she said, "Let's go on a spontaneous three-hour car trip to a luxury hotel except let's skip the luxury hotel," there's no way I would do it. I drop some gentle hints such as "Do you have to be back to your family?" and "What time is it?" and "Let's go home," but they have no effect. I'm a little bit of Denver sent right to Zachary and he's not going to let it go. Zachary is fully alive, banging on the steering wheel and eager to debate. He's railing on the Republicans' failure to repeal the Affordable Care Act: "It makes me think there's something out there. Either the insurance people are all in their pockets or the elitists are all running it." I, meanwhile, am less concerned about national policy than Zachary's policy about the length of a Sunday drive. Then, noticing either my discomfort or the fuel gauge, he turns the truck around. An hour later, we finally pull into Miami toward Snob Hill, and I thank Zachary for the tour and the talk.

But Zachary isn't pulling onto my street. Instead, he keeps driving. Fast. Past Miami. Back on the highway, going the other way. He does not address this bizarre decision, which is frightening. Especially because his Facebook photos include a pistol surrounded by the words "Now I lay me down to sleep / Beside my bed a Glock I keep / If I wake and you're inside / The coroner's van will be your last ride." I get nervous as Zachary takes us farther and farther out of town. Is he looking for an unmarked place to bury me? That seems unlikely, since every place we've passed for three hours is unmarked. Is he going to try to convert me? To kiss me? If so, do I go along with it in order to change his mind on gay marriage?

But Zachary merely wants to talk. Eventually, I coax him back to Snob Hill and he drops me off. I feel dumb for being nervous, though not as dumb as he must feel for wasting hundreds of dollars of gasoline when we could have talked over free Keurig coffees at the Cowboys and Roses. Before I get out of the truck, Zachary says that though he loves all the people of Miami, there are levels of trust even here. "There's no doubt that there are some people in this town who have money and are elites. They drive the brand-name vehicles. It's not hard to spot them. In a lot of ways, they're the best looking. They do look down on some people," he says. "I'm not going to tell them my innermost secrets." When I ask him what the social life of the Miami elite is like, he describes people I know back in Los Angeles. Specifically me. "They drink wine and eat cheese and talk down about people." Though Zachary is too nice to name the elites, I think I know where they'll be.

CHAPTER 8

The 33 Party

There are 200 people—a third of the town—in this huge open field fringed by mountains. Even though the Baptists aren't among them, I see people I know sooner than I would at a party in Los Angeles. I recognize "48," the guy who always wears a Jimmie Johnson T-shirt, though this is largely due to the fact that he's wearing a Jimmie Johnson T-shirt. He hands me a beer, which brings back memories of high school, since that's both the last time I drank beer illegally and the last time I had a Coors Light.

In a tradition since this party started in 1995, people hand over fifty dollars in exchange for the name of a randomly selected NFL team. If that team scores exactly 33 points in a game this season, they'll get a payout. There's also a raffle, despite the fact that this 33 game is also technically a raffle. In the second raffle, a woman with shoelace straps crossing over her cleavage in a way that my Baptist friends would not approve of, wins $325. She also won the raffle at the annual Cow Calling Championship in June. The prize that time was a Luger, which after four days here is starting to sound like a beautiful name for a girl. I haven't, however, been here long enough to make winning a gun in a raffle seem beautiful. The last raffle I was part of in Los Angeles was for Women Against Gun Violence.

I spot Mayor Breeding rocking his newborn twins in a double stroller. The tiny boy is wearing skinny jeans and the trompe-l'oeil-sneaker socks that are my go-to baby gift. The mayor stands next to his tall, beautiful second wife, Erin. He's mellow and humble, claiming he got tricked into the mayorship when he agreed to be an alderperson and then the mayor retired and he was next in line. Despite his story of no-conflict small-town politics, I know Miami had its own populist revolution. Breeding, who lives on one of the huge ranches out of town, lost the election for the much more powerful position of county judge to the tire shop–running, Whatever Store–owning, Table of Knowledge–presiding, Criminal Flats–residing Rick Tennant.

Before we get in line for the catered barbecue, we join hands with whomever we're near, bow our heads, and pray. Afterward, I get in line but then someone from the other end of the field who missed our prayer leads us in grace again. Instead of telling this person we already graced, we join hands again. I have held hands with more people in Miami than in every other place I've been to cumulatively. It's nice, but I'm concerned about sharing germs right before I eat. Jesus wouldn't want this. I know he cleaned a leper, but I have to imagine that he washed his hands before grabbing a sandwich. I wonder if the growth in the global Christian population is due to the fact that they spent centuries building up powerful immunities to communicable diseases.

I take a heaping plate of ribs, pork loin, sausage, corn on the cob, beans, jalapeño poppers, and peach cobbler to a picnic table with Mayor Breeding, his wife, Erin, and her brother, Mitchell Locke, both in their midthirties. Their great-great-grandfather helped found Miami, and now the Lockes own a multimillion-dollar ranch with 600 mother cows. By merging the Locke and Breeding fortunes, the mayor has consolidated his power over the kingdom, undoubtedly giving him access to the best table at the Rafter B Café.

Erin is a fast-talking, hilarious schoolteacher of kids with severe emotional needs, a job so tough her employers gave her self-defense training. She's got long brown hair and a body that moms of newborn twins are only supposed to have in Los Angeles. Mitchell, a thin guy with a trimmed hipster beard, works for their dad on the family ranch. He considered becoming a professor after getting his master's in English, the same useless degree I have.

Erin pours me an Australian chardonnay that she apologizes for, since getting decent wine is hard in this dry county. Mitchell asks me what I've found most surprising about Miami, so I tell him how my wife and mom warned me not to tell anyone that I'm Jewish. He and his sister laugh and tell me they know the dreidel song which I confirm by making them sing. Their beloved school librarian, Mrs. Lotman, was Jewish and taught them the song every Hanukkah. Erin's best college friend is Lindsay Feinberg, a Jewish journalist in Manhattan who writes for *Vice*, has her own food blog, and shares three mutual friends with me on Facebook. They have more access to my world than I do to theirs. In fact, they have more access to my world than I have to my world. Two of Erin's friends in New York are HIV positive. She and Mitchell have an adult cousin with two school-age kids who is a trans woman.

As the sun sets, Lindsay Gil, whose grandmother Janie carries around her quilting supplies in a Chivas Regal bag, joins us at the picnic table. Lindsay is a brash, funny, divorced graphic designer who makes pop art based on cow skulls and Native American images. She's wearing oversized tortoiseshell librarian glasses and animal-print clothing; she looks like she got off the F train at Carroll Street. Lindsay says she'll organize a party for me the next night so I can meet all their friends. I'm not about to move to Miami, but if I had to, I could build an enjoyable life here. Because there are elites everywhere.

We pull chairs around a movie-sized TV screen someone rented for the Mayweather–McGregor fight. The crowd's support of McGregor isn't as fervent as I anticipated, and it's hard to parse how much of their rooting is due to race. After all, people everywhere love underdogs. Besides, Mayweather is a monster, having been arrested several times for beating women. He also did not give it his all on *Dancing with the Stars*. Plus he looks unprepared, while McGregor is all vim and heart. All three judges give McGregor round one. And two. And three. The crowd laughs every time McGregor stops himself—or the ref stops him—from using a martial arts move. Thirty seconds into the seventh round, however, McGregor gasps air through his mouth, at which point Mayweather punches him in the face a lot. By the ninth round it's clear that Mayweather was letting McGregor bounce around until he got tired, like you do with a child. In the tenth round, McGregor lies against the ropes, no longer defending against the blows, and the ref calls the fight in favor of elitism. No one here seems disappointed. Possibly because McGregor put on a good show for a non-boxer. But I suspect the rest of Miami is taking the loss harder. The people here tonight know Mayweather is their elite kin.

The next night, Lindsay calls to postpone my party by a day so she can prepare. The next day she downgrades from dinner to cocktails. At the last minute, she cancels entirely due to her boyfriend's panic about his daughter, whose house was flooded in Houston. The postponing and canceling has only increased my belief that I could be friends with this clique, since this is exactly how we socialize in LA. When Angelenos say, "We should have lunch sometime," they don't mean that we will have lunch. They mean, "I like you enough that if we were in the same restaurant at the same time, I would sit with you."

My final morning in Miami, North Korea launches a missile over Japan—the second test since Jerry told me that Trump had ended these provocations with his tough talk. I consider walking over to Jerry's house and telling him, but there's no point. Not only because I won't change his mind, but also because I'm never going to see him or anyone in this town again. Which makes me sad. I'd love to come back, but I know that I have family to visit in New Jersey, Florida, and New York. And I want to take my son to Paris. And I've never been to Vienna. Korea sounds interesting. Besides, these people, none of whom I convinced of anything, will soon forget me. Jerry and his friends will never think about my elitst soul again.

I sign the Cowboys and Roses guest book, writing a positive review that plays up the breakfasts and down the scorpion infestation. I close the door behind me, which feels oddly unfinal because it's not locked and I can open it right back up. I wish I'd booked a longer stay. There are still people I want to meet. Maybe, if I stayed long enough, my elite friends would have thrown that party for me. I could have gotten the Table of Knowledge to trust me. I could have gone to the Calf Fry Cookoff tomorrow in Canadian, the town north of here, although that sounds less appealing now that I've looked it up and learned that "calf fries" are cow testicles.

I drive west on the Zachary McDowell highway, and shortly before I reach the Amarillo International Airport, I pull over alongside the road. I walk past an open gate and through 200 yards of grass. In the middle of a field, ten cars half a century old are buried halfway into the earth, their hoods pointed skyward like a message from a lost civilization. Spray-paint cans are scattered everywhere, and people pick them up to graffiti the cars all day long, mostly tagging their own names on the vehicles. A Danish guy in his twenties in cycling gear tells me he is biking alone from coast to coast across America. He's on the same journey as me, only with the opposite goal. He hasn't come to find answers or change anyone's mind. He got on his bike to shut out the news. He idly sprays a car with paint, drawing nothing in particular, adding to the layers of meaninglessness at the Cadillac Ranch.

I should have done what the Danish cyclist did.

Because I failed. I did not convince even one person in Miami of the huge mistake they've made in rejecting the elite. I want to blame this on the fact that my energy was depleted from that scorpion sting, but it's become clear that it never stung me.

Right before the airport, I drive by a row of white Cadillac limousines with longhorns mounted on their hoods. They're parked in front of the Big Texan Steak Ranch, where the seventy-two-ounce steak is free if you finish it along with the side dishes in less than an hour. Teenagers sometimes hang out in the parking lot, laughing at the people puking. It's a populist circus, where the entertainment is the excesses of the elites.

On the first leg of my flight home, I try to talk to the guy sitting next to me, like I did with everyone in Miami, but he doesn't look up from his computer. When my second flight is delayed at the Denver Airport, people complain and look at their phones instead of bonding over our potential new adventure with our free food vouchers. It's the Denver that Zachary warned me about.

When I get home from the airport, I quietly go upstairs to Laszlo's room. He's barely awake, so I lean down and gently kiss him on the cheek. He sits up, hugs me tightly, and says, "You stink."

"What do I smell like?" I ask.

"You smell like somewhere else," he says.

I smile and think, *I smell like America.*

PART II

The Elites

There is a growing disrespect for government and for churches and for schools, the news media, and other institutions.…We are at a turning point in our history. There are two paths to choose. One is a path I've warned about tonight, the path that leads to fragmentation and self-interest. Down that road lies a mistaken idea of freedom, the right to grasp for ourselves some advantage over others. That path would be one of constant conflict between narrow interests ending in chaos and immobility. It is a certain route to failure.

—Jimmy Carter,
the "Crisis of Confidence" speech, 1979

CHAPTER 9

Resistance Dinner Parties

I am walking up my block to a party, this time with a bottle of wine that isn't even from America. In the three months since the election, Stephanie's house has become busier than ever, a center of revolutionary fervor. Democratic representatives Nancy Pelosi, Maxine Waters, Ted Lieu, and Adam Schiff show up for her "Stephanie Miller Resistance Dinner Parties."

After my trip to Miami, I want to observe my fellow elites with a new perspective. Maybe our striving, global, diverse, loosely intertwined lifestyle is breaking the world into angry atoms. To find out, I'm traveling to the most elite area possible. Which, the elites will be pleased to know, will not leave any carbon footprint.

While the best place to observe nationalists was in

Miami, Texas, because they rarely leave their town, the best place to observe elites isn't in Georgetown, Palo Alto, or even my district in Los Angeles, where only 11 percent of votes were cast for Trump, mostly likely as part of an ill-conceived conceptual art project. The most elite location isn't a physical spot because we sort ourselves into buckets too tiny for a zip code; not everyone on my block is equally elite. That's why we convene at pop-up inversions of Miami, Texas, such as the party I'm going to now. While 95.3 percent of Roberts County voted for Trump, that's not as impressive as the percentage of Hillary Clinton voters at Stephanie's parties, which is 100. I do not know that for a fact, of course. It could be that one guest voted twice, bringing the figure up to 101 percent.

Unlike in Miami, where everyone knows the newcomers as soon as they move into town, I lived in my house in the Hollywood Hills for two years before meeting Stephanie, who lives four doors away. Elite Los Angeles is friendlier than elite New York, where I lived in an apartment for seven years and never knew all the people on my floor.

The only reason I met Stephanie is because the lights in our house went out early one evening. Cassandra suggested we walk around and see if the whole neighborhood lost power or if I had to pretend to try to fix something in our house. It wasn't dark enough out for us to tell from looking into peoples's windows, so when Cassandra heard people in a backyard, she rang the bell on the gate to get some information. A young guy came up and said it wasn't his house, but invited us in. This seemed an unnecessary part of our quest, but like any good member of the elite, Cassandra will not pass up an opportunity to look at real estate. We walked uphill past a pool to a patio where nearly a dozen people sat around a table, drinking white wine and recording a podcast. Three were comedians famous enough that I knew who they were. When Stephanie recognized me because of my *Time* column, she started to interview me. It was the third podcast I had been a guest on that was recorded on my block. I am including my own podcast.

Stephanie did not need electricity to record a podcast. That's partly because of batteries. But it's also because Stephanie herself is electricity. She talks quickly and gestures even more quickly, her long dark hair always a second behind her. The most shameful failure for a member of the elite is not being busy. In other parts of the country, when you ask people how they're doing they'll say, "fine," "good," or "flippin whippy." Everyone I know responds: "busy." And Stephanie is one of the busiest. I often stumble out of my house at 9:30 a.m. and see her, already finished with her workday, in yoga pants and a baseball cap, returning from a hike, biking up our street, or walking her two enormous white Great Pyrenees. An hour later, she'll go by my house again, this time talking into her phone about politics while walking back from the grocery store, which is technically legal in Los Angeles only because there has never been a test case.

Stephanie has been a member of the elite her whole life. Her father, William Miller, an excellent golfer and bridge player, was an assistant prosecutor at the Nuremberg trials, a seven-term member of the House of Representatives, chair of the National Republican Committee, and 1964 vice-presidential nominee under Barry Goldwater. Stephanie went to the University of Southern California, became a standup comedian, landed a radio show, had a late-night television talk show in the 1990s, and hosted several game shows. The *Stephanie Miller Show*, which she broadcasts from her basement, features interviews with celebrity guests, song parodies, and fart jokes; it has nearly six million daily listeners and is one of the five most important liberal talk shows, according to *Talkers Magazine*. She is a skilled host, having mastered the most important elite skill, which is networking. Her greatest trick in collecting people is making everyone feel important. Stephanie spits out compliments like a stripper. It's 9 a.m., you're in your shorts and T-shirt, unshowered, throwing out a bag of garbage, and suddenly you're handsome, smart, and sexy. Stephanie is aggressively flirty, especially with men, despite being a lesbian. Her hands are suddenly squeezing your arm, her head abruptly on your shoulder, her green eyes making contact. Once, as I was leaving her house after dinner, she said goodbye by kissing me on the lips.

* * *

Cassandra and I walk up the steps to the two lion statues guarding the first door, ring the bell, and are buzzed through. We proceed through the outdoor patio and knock on Stephanie's front door. She comes to the door wearing a silver peace sign necklace and one of the more than 100 anti-Trump T-shirts she has amassed since the election, including one designed by Martin Sheen's wife, which reads, TRUMP GRABBED MY CUNTRY. She doesn't know what happened to the bottle of Trump wine I brought to her election party: maybe it was spilled down the sink; maybe it anonymously met the fate described in a T-shirt that reads, MY LIVER CAN'T HANDLE TRUMP MUCH LONGER.

She leads us into the dining room, where she introduces us to the dozen Resistors seated around the dinner table. She does this in the manner that all great elites do, which is as if they are hosting a late-night talk show. She calls me "the famous, hilarious columnist for *Time* magazine." Everyone is some Mad Libs of the adjective "brilliant," "successful," "talented," or "beautiful" followed by the noun "actor," "lawyer," "professor," "writer," "comedian," or "host." Harold didn't do this when he introduced everyone on Baptist Row. He didn't say, "This is the brilliant Larry McReynolds, Miami's second-best band-sawer of crosses out of Reader's Digest Condensed Books!"

As caterers serve the non-vegans among us salmon, we discuss national politics. The first difference I notice from Miami is the speed and volume of our conversation. I have never been part of a more heated conversation in which everyone agrees. Eventually, the dinner transforms into a question-and-answer with Malcolm Nance, a former navy officer specializing in cryptology, who is a counterterrorism analyst for NBC News and the author of *The Plot to Hack America: How Putin's Cyberspies and WikiLeaks Tried to Steal the 2016 Election*. Malcolm repeatedly says he has confidential intelligence that he can't share, and then shares it anyway couched with the terms "maybe," "rhymes with," or "an organization in Langley, Virginia." At first I figured the navy must have been annoyed that his codes were so easy to break. Then I realized that asking an elite not to tell you everything he knows is like asking an elite not to be elite.

The brilliant, four-time Golden Globe–nominated director Rob Reiner asks Malcolm a bunch of detailed questions about Washington rumors, leading Malcolm to strongly imply that there is indeed a tape of Trump paying Russian prostitutes to urinate on each other. Talented actor Ron Perlman, multi-platinum-album-selling recording artist Moby, glamorous superstar lawyer Lisa Bloom, and hilarious comedy duo Frangela all nod seriously. They are sure that once Americans learn about this video, they will be so disgusted that Trump will have to resign. They are clearly not keeping up with trends in pornography. Over dessert, we debate the technicalities of how Trump will be either impeached, convicted, or removed by his own cabinet, one of which everyone at the table assumes is inevitable. "Trust me, we will have a part and a tay when this shitshow is over," Stephanie says. A significant amount of time is devoted to how to fight the agenda of President Mike Pence.

All of this seems insane. A few months after voting for him, Americans aren't going to take extraordinary actions to get rid of a president who is acting precisely like he did on the campaign trail. I politely suggest that Trump isn't some isolated malignant mole that can be sliced off but rather part of an authoritarian cancer spreading throughout the world. This sounds sufficiently Trump-hating to me, but my denial that America has been swindled does not endear me to Rob Reiner, which sucks, because Rob Reiner endearment is the sole reason I came. It's also not making me popular with anyone else at this table, each of whom is looking at me violently. My comments did less to change their position on impeachment than on capital punishment. I am about to explain that I was so anti-Trump I registered as a Republican in order to vote for Ted Cruz in the primary, but then I realize this will make them angrier. The people here aren't as willing to withstand dissent as the people in Miami. I would not feel comfortable telling anyone here my opinion about abortion, which I think is morally wrong except in cases of rape, incest, or me accidentally getting a woman pregnant.

They go back to discussing how Russian bots tricked voters and how if middle-class voters were better educated, they wouldn't vote against their own interests. I know if voters in Miami heard this conversation, they would find a way to vote for Trump twice.

I stay as quiet as I can for the rest of the meal, trying not to offend. Being right is not worth being crossed off the guest list. I have worked too hard to get to this table to blow it now.

CHAPTER 10

The Loop

I have devoted my life to one thing. That thing probably should have been helping others. Instead I have been laser focused on becoming a member of the elite.

When I was seven, my parents took me from our suburban New Jersey town to a French restaurant in Manhattan, where they tried to dissuade me from ordering escargot by telling me that escargot are snails. It was a good strategy, but it didn't work. I suffered through those gastropods, and then I suffered through homework and extracurriculars to get into a college with brand recognition.

I got to Stanford, where I finally saw the elite in person. But I didn't get to experience being an elite until the summer I interned in Manhattan at *Newsweek* magazine. Editors handed me stray invites: a press pass to the Democratic convention, a movie screening of *Glengarry Glen Ross*, a book party at a drag queen–filled nightclub in a former church that no one in Miami, Texas, would have enjoyed except Jodye Tarpley. I went back to college knowing that if I could once again score invitations to these events, my life would be bigger, my curiosity more sated, my passed plates of hors d'oeuvres more free. I called this world where influential people congregated the Loop, and I vowed to get in.

After graduating, I landed an interview with Martha Stewart to write for her first TV show. Before we ordered lunch at an expensive Italian restaurant in Westport, Connecticut, she asked if I wanted San Pellegrino. I told her that I didn't know what San Pellegrino was. She laughed. I told her that I really didn't know what San Pellegrino was. She laughed again. This went on for longer than you would think, with me wondering if San Pellegrino was pasta, wine, or some kind of birdbath made from Popsicle sticks. She ordered San Pellegrino from the waiter, and a few minutes later, I discovered that it is a sparkling water from Italy that was a little disappointing after all that buildup.

In the year that I worked for her, I learned that the walls of the Loop were thick, and the semiotics of the club members consisted of words like *semiotics*. The Loop had its own jargon that included *carpaccio, DUMBO, omakase, St. Barths, decanter, Birkin bag,* oolong, *Fresh Air*, *Pilates*, *Uffizi*, *McKinsey & Company*, *Philippe Starck*, *Hampton Jitney*, *Talk of the Town*, *lawyered up*, and *San Pellegrino*. I tried my best to learn them.

After two years of low-level magazine fact-checking jobs, I was hired as an editor for a new magazine called *Time Out New York*. It was enough to get me on the fringes of the Loop, and I grabbed on. I turned no entrance to the Loop down, going to movie premieres, Rangers playoff games, restaurant openings, and dance performances, even though I do not like dance performances. At the book party for David Foster Wallace's *Infinite Jest*, George Plimpton asked me which one was Wallace, which I was able to answer since Wallace was wearing his trademark bandanna and trademark look of being the least happy person in the room. The happiest person in the room was the one answering literary questions for George Plimpton.

I called this velvet-roped life the Loop because I had not yet read the 1944 Memorial Lecture given by C. S. Lewis at King's College London in which he dubbed it "the Ring." A Christian apologetic, chair of Medieval and Renaissance Literature at Cambridge, and author of *The Lion, the Witch and the Wardrobe*, Lewis was less shallow than I was:

In all men's lives at certain periods, and in many men's lives at all periods between infancy and extreme old age, one of the most dominant elements is the desire to be inside the local Ring and the terror of being left outside....Has the desire to be on the right side of that invisible line ever prompted you to any act or word on which, in the cold small hours of a wakeful night, you can look back with satisfaction? If so your case is more fortunate than most....The quest of the Inner Ring will break your hearts unless you break it.

I don't understand how Lewis could think this. Avoiding the Loop is the equivalent of telling those kids not to walk through the wardrobe. The Loop offers adventure, challenges, new perspectives, and significant financial savings if you stand by the kitchen and nab enough passed appetizers to skip dinner.

Nearly all the fascinating people I've met, the places I've visited, and the money I have came from getting on the right side of that invisible line. If I had the choice between getting in the Loop and writing those six boring Narnia books after *The Lion, the Witch and the Wardrobe*, I'd totally take the Loop.

The closest I come to the center of the Loop is when I go to elite conferences. There are so many of these that a member of the elite could sell their home and live in conference hotels, flying from Davos to TED to the Aspen Ideas Festival to Bilderberg to Sun Valley, like a Deadhead who replaced Jerry Garcia with Eric Schmidt. This traveling circus is the infinitely dense dot of elite energy. The populist equivalent would be if every McReynoldses' porch in every small town were squeezed into one resort hotel ballroom. Each elite conference is like one of Stephanie's dinner parties if it were expanded to hundreds of people and they all stayed for days, eating, sleeping, and drinking in the same small space. If you want to judge the utility and the morality of elites, you have to come to an elite conference and observe them in their natural habitat.

I have never turned an invitation to an elite conference down. I've been to Reboot, where about sixty Jews are given a free three-day trip to the Stein Eriksen resort near Salt Lake City to discuss how to reinvent Judaism and briefly double the number of Jews in Utah. I took a free trip to Newcastle for that year's meeting of the British American Project, which tries to get Americans and Brits to overcome their vast differences and has many important members such as the Baron Mandelson, the Baron Robertson of Port Ellen, the Baroness Symons, the Baroness Scotland, and a woman who ran a brothel in Portugal she inherited from her father. I went to the Influencers Dinner, at which a dozen people keep their names and jobs secret until the end of the evening, at which point everyone relaxes because they're no longer wondering if they were wasting their time talking to someone. This dinner led to an invitation to the Rising Glen Collective, which was described as "TED meets pool party." I went to the Summit, a conference of 3,500 mostly under-forty elites that has become so popular that the organization purchased the largest ski resort in America and is turning it into a members-only, 500-home town in Utah. At the Aspen Institute, I tossed my return-flight ticket after scoring a ride home in a billionaire's private jet. At a panel called "Membership Has Its Privileges" at the Vanity Fair New Establishment Summit, I heard the moderator tell the CEOs of the Soho House, the dating site Raya, and the women's co-working space The Wing, "What you do well and I encourage you to do more is defend your exclusivity." I took the stage at TEDx Stanford after a woman spoke about inventing a hand-cranked phototherapy machine to save jaundiced babies in third-world rural communities without hospitals. I began my speech with the sentence "This is my son's penis." Elites are true believers in diversity.

Even people who approve of elites, such as Cassandra, are repulsed by elite conferences, the way that birdwatchers would get freaked out if 150 gulls landed in their backyard and all squawked at once about how happiness improves productivity. This revulsion to elite organizations is so strong that the most famous ones—Davos, the Council on Foreign Relations, the Trilateral Commission, Bilderberg, Bohemian Grove—are the target of conspiracy theories. In 2013, Public Policy Polling found that 28 percent of voters, undoubtedly thinking about these conferences, say they believe "a secretive power elite with a globalist agenda is conspiring to eventually rule the world."

This is idiocy. We already rule the world. And we are in no way secretive about it. Elites cannot keep a secret. You want a secret kept, you do not share it with a group of people whose value is based on networking ability. The elite have managed to keep one secret in the last fifty years: the identity of Deep Throat in the Watergate scandal. The only reason Bob Woodward, Carl Bernstein, and Ben Bradlee were able to do this was because Deep Throat was W. Mark Felt. If Deep Throat been anyone even a tiny bit more interesting than W. Mark Felt, everyone would have known by 1975. It is infinitely more interesting to say, "I cannot reveal who Deep Throat is" than to say "W. Mark Felt." Even if you are W. Mark Felt.

Conspiracy theories appeal to populists because they simplify. They blame villains for random horrors. Psychological studies show that people who feel a lack of control over their lives or the world are more likely to believe conspiracy theories, which offer a simple reason for their lack of agency. They also empower them. The conspiracist gets to be Sherlock Holmes, piecing together tiny clues to solve a crime committed by a small, corrupt group. This group is always the Jews. I know this because we talked about it at the Reboot conference in Utah.

Besides the fear that we're meeting to rig the system, people find elitist groups suspect because organizations of every kind have become uncommon, and therefore mysterious. A shrinking number of people regularly go to churches, town meetings, or extended family gatherings. At the beginning of the twentieth century, about half of adult males belonged to a fraternal organization, such as the Freemasons, the Knights of Pythias, or the Independent Order of Odd Fellows, an organization that included both my poor Jewish grandfather in the Bronx and six US presidents, all of whom joined despite the fact that one of the club's six main purposes is to "bury the dead." And not in a cool, biker gang, threatening kind of way. They actually help with funerals. This is probably how the group got their name.

Since the 1950s, these clubs have fallen away: the Kiwanis is down 40 percent, the Lions are 60 percent smaller, the Masons shrank over 70 percent, and the Odd Fellows have only 1,413 Instagram followers even though they have rigorously avoided posting pictures of fetid cadavers. Not only have these organizations shrunk, but so have the members themselves because they are all very old. When these institutions crumbled, most people didn't replace them, instead spending more time at home. But the elites built bespoke organizations for themselves.

Elite conferences take place at luxury hotels in cool places that we never get to see because we're in meetings. Cassandra cannot believe anyone would choose to spend their vacation going to meetings. Meetings are something people complain about even when they're getting paid to go to them. Most of these people at these conferences have the money to do whatever they want over their vacations—ski the Alps, scuba in the Maldives, come to these same luxury resorts and not sit in windowless conference rooms. What Cassandra doesn't understand is how much elites love a meeting. Our instinctual response to any problem is a cheery, "Let's schedule a meeting!" We have work meetings, family meetings, and board meetings. When two of us get together to eat before 11:00 a.m., we call it a breakfast meeting.

My favorite thing about an elite conference is the name tags. No one in Miami, Texas, needed a name tag, and not simply because most of them were named Dee Ann. They had only 600 names to memorize, whereas being elite entails knowing so many people that, like many attendees at an elite conference, I have exhausted Facebook's limit of 5,000 friends. When you have thousands of loose connections, greetings are stressful. Which is why every elite conference requires participants to wear name tags the entire time. I wish everyone wore name tags all the time. Names are unmemorable, meaningless sounds assigned before birth. I can't remember the names of cars, and experts are paid to come up with the perfect phonemes to evoke each model. Yet if I say, "Is that an Elantra?" no one yells, "You've met my car three times! It's Altima!"

Thanks to the name tags, I'm always reminded that I

already know a fair number of people at these conferences, partly because some of them went to Stanford with me. Despite our championing for diversity, it's rare to find an elite who didn't attend a top-ranked university. Our success is largely based on who we were before we turned eighteen. If dating worked the same way, nearly every member of the elite would still be single.

While most of the attendees at elite conferences have attended exclusive colleges, we are not all rich. Money is not a primary motivation for the elite. We are far more into impressing each other than into making money. The elite dream is not to own a yacht but to give a TED talk. In 1918's *The Education of Henry Adams*—an autobiography so elitist that it was written in third person—the grandson of a president and great-grandson of another wrote:

> Newspapers might prate about wealth till commonplace print was exhausted, but as a matter of habit, few Americans envied the rich for anything the most of them got out of money. New York might occasionally fear them, but more often laughed or sneered at them, and never showed them respect. Scarcely one of the very rich men held any position in society by virtue of his wealth, or could have been elected to an office, or even into a good club.

Most rich people are not elite. They live far from the nation's cultural centers and run boring businesses. One rich guy I met owned a bunch of truck stop motels in Texas, another made a part for gas pumps, and a third owned a lot of Arby's in Omaha. You could own all the Arby's in Omaha and you'd never be elite, unless you were already Warren Buffett, smoked weed, and got the munchies so bad that you bought all the local Arby's. Donald Trump is a billionaire and was never invited to Davos until he became president. Though he went to the University of Pennsylvania and donated enough to politicians to attend social functions in New York, including Chelsea Clinton's wedding, it was his singular focus on making money no matter how crass the venture—teaching Learning Annex classes, starting Trump University, selling Trump Vodka—that kept him outside the elite.

Half of the attendees at elite conferences aren't rich. They're academics, journalists, artists, government employees, politicians, and people who work at charities, a word we find so distastefully unimportant sounding we call them "nongovernmental organizations." There's a priest at one conference I go to who has taken a vow of poverty. I don't know what kind of workaround he's devised for staying at a $300-a-night oceanfront resort, but I assume he dutifully removes his mattresses and sleeps directly on the box spring. The richest attendee at any of the conferences I go to is Silicon Valley venture capitalist and LinkedIn cofounder Reid Hoffman, a multibillionaire who, according to *Forbes*, is the 703rd wealthiest person on earth, but he doesn't care much about money. He's driven the same Audi for nearly ten years, lived in the same four-bedroom house, and taken the Giving Pledge created by Warren Buffett and Bill Gates to donate half his money to charity. If I were the 703rd richest person in the world, I'd have way more fun with my fortune, constantly calling up the 704th person and offering him wads of cash to drink a jar of pickle juice. Making money wasn't Reid's goal. He planned on becoming a professor, studying philosophy at Oxford on a Marshall scholarship. He got rich by being really smart and being at Stanford at the perfect time. Which was the same time as me. So mostly the smart thing.

Far more than money, Reid loves an elite conference. He goes to about a dozen every year and has even cofounded one. Which has helped establish him as an elite; connector of the elite; the headline of the *New Yorker* profile of him is "The Network Man." Reid is so elite that he is one of about a hundred non-Brits in history to be named an Honorary Commander of the Most Excellent Order of the British Empire, which gives him the power to approach Turkish businesswoman Suzan Sabanci Dinçer at any party and say, "Hey, I think we're both Honorary Commanders of the Most Excellent Order of the British Empire."

At one conference I went to with Reid, attendees

were split up into small assigned groups so we could go around a table and share our current passion. People were struggling to pick only one, while I struggled to come up with a passion I could pretend to have. This was particularly stressful because I was sitting next to Reid, who has no lack of passions. One of which is being nice. When he was on the cover of *Venture Capital Journal* magazine, which in my opinion is the premier journal of venture capital, the cover line was "Nice Guys *Can* Finish First." He talks slowly and earnestly, spending most of his time listening; many people call him the Yoda of Silicon Valley. He's mastered that Stephanie Miller trick of complimenting everyone, turning it into a business philosophy he calls "make everyone a hero in their own story." Reid even looks like a nice guy: pale, doughy, stubbly, schlumpy, and smiley. If people used the word "kempt" they would not use it with Reid.

When it was his turn, Reid told our table that he wants to reboot the board game Life to make it about the real decisions people make as they grow up. For my passion I went with "I'm passionate about finding a passion." A Silicon Valley guy told me that I could share his passion, which was virtual reality. I took him up on his offer and wrote a cover story about it for *Time*, but it stopped being my passion when I was halfway done writing it. I am still, after all these years, a faker and a striver among the elite, a pretender in the Loop.

The one time I got to bring Cassandra as a fellow

elite conference participant, she hated it even more than she thought she would. "The self-important pompousness of it all is kind of astounding," she said. "It feels like the Justice League. Like they think, 'We're going to change the world,' when ultimately they're just jacking off. I literally heard people saying things like 'How are we going to bring this into the world?' Who are you? The UN? What makes you think that because someone is the CEO of whatever that they're going to change the world?" This confused me. Who does Cassandra think changes the world if not CEOs, mayors, senators, venture capitalists, and people in the military, all of whom were there? Even more confusing, her guess is apparently the United Nations.

I bring Cassandra's concerns to Reid, who listens thoughtfully before saying, "A network of intelligence and voices is how all decision-making works." Reid made his career out of this belief, first founding one of the earliest social networks and then cofounding LinkedIn. His first investment was in the proto-Facebook social network Friendster. After that he invested in the social networks Flickr, Groupon, and Facebook.

This has been Reid's philosophy since he was thirteen. Upset with all the suffering in the world, he came up with a plan to save it. He got each of his friends to agree to attain a different leadership position. One would be president, one would be CEO of IBM, and he'd be director of the CIA. Then they'd use their mutual trust to create a better, kinder structure for the planet.

Reid has a map on his office wall that is as symbolic of his faith as the fifteen dining room crosses are to Larry McReynolds's. It's a map free of nations or physical distance. It's a map of relationships. It has a dot in the center, with Reid's name next to it. Thousands of lines radiate out from it to dots representing all the people he's connected to via LinkedIn, and each of their dots connects to their connections. His dot is the densest, like a universe in the midst of creating itself. He's the equivalent of the guy in your town who has a guy for everything: a hubcap guy, a football-tickets guy, a Cuban-cigar guy. Only Reid has a United-Nations-secretary-general guy, a former-president guy, a senator guy, and a CEO-of-Facebook guy. The map is the nerd equivalent of a wall of framed photographs of him with famous people. But it communicates Reid's guiding thesis that people need to make personal appeals in order to accomplish anything. And personal appeals work better when you're at a luxury hotel providing free alcohol.

To shoot out his dot's lines further, Reid makes his social connections diverse. Even though he's a lifelong liberal (as a kid in Berkeley, his parents took him to protests where he ingested tear gas), he was college buddies with libertarian billionaire Peter Thiel, who spoke at the Republican convention in favor of Trump.

After they graduated, they cohosted a public access show where they argued about politics. One of their disagreements was over a Margaret Thatcher quote that Peter loved. She was answering the same question Jerry asked me at Bible study about how to help a homeless person. My answer was that society should do it. Thatcher's answer was, "Who is society? There is no such thing! There are individual men and women, and there are families. No government can do anything except through people. And people look to themselves first."

Cassandra thinks all of the lines we added to our graph by going to an annual elite conference together are too thin to matter because we're likely to see most of the attendees only once a year. I find this a strange argument, since she sees her parents twice a year. But I see her point: this isn't Miami, Texas. There is a trade-off. Reid can have so many connections partly because he doesn't have kids. Every night the Odd Fellows spend burying the dead is one fewer they spend tucking their kids in.

But even in Miami not all lines can be equally thick. The connections I make at conferences are indeed secondary, but they're valuable. The happiness of a friend of a friend of a friend — whom you might never meet — increases your happiness three times more than a $5,000 raise. We're all connected. That's why Reid's map doesn't include only the lines coming from his dot, but also the ones connecting his connections.

Despite Cassandra's belief that only the UN can get anything done, these conferences do effect change. "Take criminal justice as an issue," Reid says. "The only way I would get exposed to this is people asking me for money, and I would ignore it. Yet when I sit down at one of these events with Van Jones and he says, 'This is a modern face of racism and you should be helping,' I can say, 'This is a big issue for some people but don't more people die from problems in health care?' He says, 'Sure. But do we want to be racist?'" In conversations about geopolitics at Bilderberg, Reid says he can sometimes offer a tech solution that political and military experts haven't considered. "You're talking about whether there's going to be a war with North Korea. What are the angles of a peaceful solution? I say, 'Maybe this one piece of technology might be useful to you guys,'" he explains. Reid stresses that the North Korea conversation is hypothetical and never happened. This makes me sure that Reid knows about a piece of technology that can help with North Korea, and it's probably a robot assassin that looks like Dennis Rodman.

I thought the Stephanie Miller Resistance Dinner Parties were merely elites comforting each other, but she later told me that the guests helped each other with donating, campaigning, and crafting messages for interviews. Rob Reiner wrote the foreword for Malcolm Nance's next book. Cassandra was wrong when she said the elite conference attendees were "just jacking off." Despite weird rumors I've heard about fraternities, I don't believe you are ever jacking off when you're in a group.

At one elite conference, I attend a session called "Why Do People Love Dictators?" The conversation turns to populism, so I ask the ten people in the conference room why the people in Miami, Texas, would think this conference is a scheme to keep power from them.

One person suggests it's a failure of messaging. We need to let them know that we are spending our vacations in meetings in windowless conference rooms to figure out how to improve their lives by making the world a better place. In the session right on the other side of this partition wall, people with money, political power, engineering skills, and lines shooting every which way from their dots are discussing how to bring technology jobs to small towns.

But people in Miami do not want a rural Silicon Valley. They want their way of life to thrive, not to live in cave wall shadows of our world. "What do you think the people in Miami, Texas, would call those people next door?" I ask.

They're quiet for a second. Then someone says it: "Missionaries."

We don't need the people in Miami to code. We don't need them to become elite. Or even like the elite. We simply need them to believe in the necessity of our expertise. We need to show what a disaster it would be if I switched places with any of the people at this conference.

One of the most dangerous populist ideas—the one proposed by people like Jerry and Judge Rick Tennant—is that politicians don't need any experience. That guts and common sense are all it takes.

I'm the perfect person to disprove that theory. I have some guts. I have some common sense. And I definitely have no experience.

Puppet Pig

In a very Reid Hoffman move, Los Angeles mayor Eric Garcetti invited me to dinner three months after I moved to the city in 2005. We'd never met, but we had three mutual friends, and those were unnecessary strings that the then city council member could snip and connect directly to his dot. I liked Eric immediately. Mostly because he's similar to me. He's a Jew who is exactly my age, and looks so much like me that at the 2008 Democratic convention, he texted me that several people had walked up to him thinking he was me. This didn't seem to bode well for his political career.

Other than our age, religion, looks, and attending both the conference I went to with Reid and Reboot, Eric and I have nothing in common. He, for instance, has accomplished an amazing amount, whereas I work from home and spend much of my day deciding when to shower. The son of LA's former district attorney, Eric speaks perfect Spanish, was a Rhodes Scholar, studied for a PhD at the London School of Economics, was an assistant professor at Occidental College, serves as a lieutenant in the Navy Reserve, fostered seven children, plays jazz piano, and was on the LA City Council for twelve years, including six as its president. Every single photo of him online verifies that he has showered, and that he knew exactly when to do it, which was right away.

Eric is the anti-Trump. He's low-key and self-effacing, preferring to negotiate complicated long-term solutions through compromise behind closed doors. The theme for his first administration was Back to Basics. He spends a fair amount of time working on fixing potholes. As I heard him say to the audience at the Vanity Fair New Establishment Summit, "You can't bullshit a pothole. It's either filled or not. It's not just tweeting and retweeting." While populists like Trump constantly search for a win to celebrate, Eric circumvents battles. He can do this because he's nurtured relationships over decades in government. He is always working on the longest term possible; uneaten metaphorical marshmallows pile up on his desk. The main wall of his office is decorated with a huge Ed Ruscha oil painting of Los Angeles at night superimposed with the words FASTER THAN A BEANSTALK, which sums up his governing philosophy.

I text Eric and ask if I can be mayor of Los Angeles for a day. I consider lying that I have cancer, but I refrain. He asks me what I mean by my request, which is a brilliant way of saying no. I explain that I'd like to follow him for a day, make each of the decisions he's confronted with, and then have him tell me if they're the same as the ones he came up with. His reaction to this ridiculous request is to text "Sure."

It's early on a Thursday morning, but Eric is glad to see me, like he's glad to see everyone, like he's glad to be everywhere. He told me he picked today for my fake mayorship because there would be lots of action, which seems dubious since we're about to go to an MTA board meeting, where he presides as chair once a month. I will be pretend-voting on fifty-one items, outlined in a nineteen-page agenda. These items involve $120 billion worth of transportation outlined on a spreadsheet that I find dizzying in its complexity, especially since I cannot think in billions of dollars. Like if someone asked, "Do you think this thing is worth a billion dollars?" I would always say no unless it were a billion-dollar bill. More insane, this is a forty-year plan. I am the same age as Eric, and my forty-year plan is to be dead.

The Los Angeles County Metropolitan Transportation Authority is housed in a gorgeous, twenty-five-floor art deco building I have never heard of. Eric sits in the middle of a half-circle desk with fifteen other board members in front of an enormous room filled with 150 spectators. Behind this semicircle desk are two more semicircle desks full of administrators. These all face a desk where three people can testify on each item. It looks less like we are going to vote on bus driver salaries and more like we're going to hear Stephanie Miller's dad argue that we should execute Nazis.

I have no idea how I would vote on any of the fifty-one items. Subject 2017-0629, which requires a two-thirds vote, would purchase a production rail tamper for $3,378,292. I have no idea if that's a good price for a rail tamper, if the county truly needs a rail tamper, or what a rail tamper is. All I know is that it is a very specific price for anything, making those tenths of a cent they charge for gas seem reasonable. We're also going to have two different votes on brake system overhauls, which I am totally voting for. There's no way I'd be the mayor who is blamed for deaths due to un-overhauled brakes.

I'm staring at my spreadsheet, trying to figure out how to vote on "light rail vehicle midlife modernization program consultant support services for specification development & solicitation of contractor," when my phone buzzes. It's a text from Eric, who is twenty feet in front of me and seems like he's paying attention to the expert panelists advising the board about a construction bid. The text says:

Now the fun begins. Puppet pig

I am annoyed that there is yet more transportation jargon: rail tampers, specification development, puppet pigs. Then a man approaches the lectern to give public comment. He is holding a pig puppet adorned with a red dress. In a high-pitched voice I do not associate with pigs, the puppet offers a detailed, extremely positive opinion about the board's work. The mayor treats both puppet and puppeteer respectfully, thanking them for their comments. This is particularly impressive since a year earlier the puppeteer had handed in a speaker request card to a black city council member on which he had drawn a burning cross next to a Ku Klux Klan member calling him the n-word. When a restraining order was filed against him, the puppeteer had to turn in several pistols, a rifle, and an unregistered AK-47. If I knew any of this right now instead of weeks later when I will Google this, I would run out of the buildling while urinating in my pants. Tabloid newspaper headlines would have read THIS LITTLE PIGGY MADE THE MAYOR GO WEE WEE WEE ALL THE WAY HOME.

When the meeting finally ends, Eric is approached by a small group of reporters. They do not ask him much about the meeting. As a journalist, I know why: that meeting was boring. Instead they ask him about today's biggest national story, which involves sexual harassment. I would have responded to their questions by saying I didn't harass anyone. This is not what Real Mayor does. Eric uses the question as an opportunity to provide instructions on filing harassment complaints through city services. I think the reason he's doing better than I am at mayoring is that he knows how the government works.

I follow Eric to the parking lot, where his driver takes us to City Hall in his black Yukon SUV. I ask the mayor and City Councilmember Paul Krekorian, who has bummed a ride with us, if they know what a rail tamper is. Eric looks at me thoughtfully, as if he's about to give me a long lecture on the complexities of running a huge city and all the details you have to master. But instead he says, "OK, Google, what is a rail tamper?" His phone teaches all three of us that a rail tamper is a machine that presses those rocks around train tracks into the ground. I am feeling more like I could be mayor. Also, that I'd be willing to press rocks down with my feet for $3,378,292. One thing I'd need to improve my mayoring is Borja Leon, a civil engineer who was at Eric's side during the meeting today. Borja is Eric's transportation secretary and supervises four employees, all of whom know what a rail tamper is. I'd need Borjas for all my meetings. Being mayor of LA is like running a portfolio of thirty-six corporations encompassing more than 40,000 employees, including police, fire, water and power, parks, ports, and the zoo. Each of these companies has its own CEO, and some are more important than others, such as the one where all the employees have guns.

We park at City Hall, and head to the mayor's huge

office, where he works at a long table instead of a desk, since he's nearly always meeting with people. An assistant hands him a stack of papers to sign, and I look through them, realizing it would take me hours to figure out what they're about. Eric says he probably doesn't know what they're about, either. But as he signs them he offers an excuse for why he happens to know about each one: he worked with that nonprofit; he's the one hiring this employee; he pushed for this gas pipeline. "A lot of people think what politicians do is exercise good or bad judgment," he says. "There's a prejudice in the profession that this isn't a craft like being a CEO or an electrician or a juggler. Government is more complicated than a business, which has a simpler set of objectives. And it takes you a long time to get good at it." Trump, he says, is steering a truck without a commercial driver's license, and we're all crammed into the trailer. Also, he's not looking at the road because he's on his phone tweeting.

There's a bearable lightness to Eric's way of looking at leadership not as a battle against evil but as a series of engineering challenges. When I ask Eric why he's signing with a cheap pen while the dinky charity for used-furniture equipment signed their side of the document with an embossed seal, he gives the problem some thought. After a moment, he reaches across his desk and picks up a gigantic pink pen topped with a fuzzy-haired Troll.

A staffer removes the signed papers, and for the first

time today, we are alone. Eric says he likes to use this rare spare time to write, which is a dick thing to say because writing is what I do in my not-spare time. In the middle of writing on a pad with a smile on his face—something I've only seen done by writers on television shows—he happily says of this lazy afternoon, "Most days I realize it's 3:00 p.m. and I haven't peed." I am grateful for this observation, since it's nearly 3:00 p.m. and I've only urinated twice since I woke up. I've been looking for an opportunity, and now, finally, we will take a break and get to it. I place my hands on my chair's armrests and start to get up, but the mayor gets right back to writing. Who talks about peeing and then doesn't pee? This is like when Cassandra once said to me, "Speaking of sex, did you hear this week's *This American Life*?" Instead of using his spare time to conduct necessary bodily functions, the mayor plays his voicemails, which he hasn't done in a week. This is an activity that I know from personal experience can be accomplished while urinating. Even if one of the voicemails is from the governor.

At 3:00 p.m., our bladders still full, we head to a room marked CENTCOM packed with about fifty people. This is clearly a fake meeting, created for me. People sit in front of placards that say things such as CHIEF OF POLICE and FIRE CHIEF. There's a guy in charge of sanitation. It's as if Laszlo created a mayor's Central Command meeting out of Legos. I'm even more suspicious of Laszlo's involvement when I notice that the shelves are lined with immaculate dioramas of toy buses, police cars, garbage trucks, ambulances, and fire trucks in action. There are two screens in the front of the room, showing maps and bar charts, which all the uniformed people look at intently. It feels as if we are going to discuss how to handle the city's brash new superhero.

We are here to discuss homelessness, which is even more complicated than transportation. The group is collecting data from two small homeless encampments. The homeless downtown are older, long-term opioid addicts who grew up nearby, many now with mental health issues. The ones in Hollywood near my house are young runaways from around the country, many of whom are gay, and they often do meth. They cause different problems, have different needs, and have built different communities. During this ninety-minute meeting with no bathroom breaks, the mayor doesn't make one decision. No one asks where to build a shelter, or if he should arrest people in tents, or what to do with the 802 pounds of human waste homeless people leave each week on the streets of Hollywood that, as I cross my legs and squirm in my seat, I can totally empathize with. Instead, Eric gets the people in this room to work together and share information. This requires not only knowing how all the parts of the city government work, but also being able to call key players not in this room. The job is knowing people. It's how Reid Hoffman said decision-making works.

The mayor invites me out to dinner with his wife, Amy, and their five-year-old daughter, Maya, whom they got through a foster program in order to make me feel worse about myself. I figure we're going to a steak joint full of lobbyists, where Maya will cough from cigar smoke, whiskey fumes, and the rancid smell of corruption. Instead, Eric's driver takes us to Plan Check, a local burger chain. We walk inside and no one seems to notice us. This is weird because one of us is the mayor and the other one looks so much like the mayor he could be a body double if security were necessary for a politician no one recognizes.

Eric looks at a text from Amy telling him what to order for them and reviews the menu. I have had enough. I sprint to the bathroom and urinate for so long I worry about missing dinner because the mayor will have to leave to deal with an emergency caused by the sewer pipe I burst. Meanwhile, the mayor orders burgers for me and his family, watches a bit of the Cowboys-Redskins game on the TV above the bar, and then goes to the bathroom as if it's a way to kill time. He explains that not urinating is not a genetic ability but learned from decades of sitting through endless meetings. "I have a completely flat ass," he explains.

As we eat, I show Maya a photo of her father signing legislation with the Trolls pen. "I have the same pen," she says. I inform her gently that the city has claimed eminent domain over her Trolls pen. She nods much like her dad, as if this is a problem she can solve. I get the feeling she is lawyered up.

After dinner, the mayor goes to speak at a fundraiser for the homeless. Sitting in the greenroom before Eric speaks, I overhear a rock band talking about whether they should go inside to hear Obama. They are acting very cool about this, even for a rock band. I don't see Secret Service around, but when I open the back door to the theater, I indeed see Barack Obama onstage, flanked by two Secret Service agents. If you're wondering if it's strange for the mayor of Los Angeles to come onstage after a Barack Obama impersonator, I can confirm that it is. Fake Obama points at Real Eric Garcetti in the audience and begs him to run for president to continue Real Obama's legacy. I agree, not only due to Eric's qualifications, intelligence, and demeanor, but also because I would make bank as a President Garcetti impersonator.

At 8:00 p.m., Eric heads home, ending nearly a twelve-hour day, during which I have seen him go to the bathroom twice. Before he gets in the Yukon, I ask him how I would do as mayor. "I think you would start strong and flame out with a scandal. Because of all the temptation," he says about his mundane day. Eric's security guy drops me off at the now empty parking lot underneath the huge Metropolitan Transportation Authority Building. He's former military, and it seems like he's not a fan of the elite. But he likes the way his boss respects everyone and handles problems calmly. It's what an elite member of the military would do.

As I drive home, I feel safer than I have in a while. While few of the politicians I've met have the equanimity that Eric does, almost all of them were problem-solvers like him. The populists have not won, as I feared on election night. There are still more of us in power than them. Ironically, by "us" I mean people who don't think in terms of us-and-them.

Still, I worry that "us" is shrinking, because some of "us" are joining "them."

There are traitors among us.

PART III

The Populist Elites

In most of the operations of the mind each American appeals only to the individual effort of his own understanding...they are constantly brought back to their own reason as the most obvious and proximate source of truth. It is not only confidence in this or that man which is destroyed, but the disposition to trust the authority of any man whatsoever. Everyone shuts himself up tightly within himself and insists upon judging the world from there.

Alexis de Tocqueville,
Democracy in America, *1840*

CHAPTER 12

Dilbert

I turn my phone on as soon as my flight lands in Oakland and see this text:

> My startup makes this app
> that lets people track each
> other on the way to meet.
> Please join my Approach
> https://geostre.am/exbqcv/0

Downloading the app does not seem like a good idea, since it would let a traitor track my every movement. Not downloading it, however, seems like telling *Dilbert* cartoonist Scott Adams that I don't trust him. Besides, my fears about Miami, Texas, were proven to be irrational. This trip is even less threatening, because, while there have been a lot of murdered cartoonists, there hasn't been one cartoonist murderer. Which is surprising, since they seem to enjoy drawing characters firing guns twisted in spirals in such a way that they shoot themselves in the face. I'm also placated by the fact that Scott gave me his home address, which is a bigger security compromise than downloading an app.

Scott watches me drive twenty-five miles in my rental car to his home in Pleasanton, a town named after the fact that it is pleasant. It is the charming, old-fashioned village that Miami, Texas, wants to be. It has an adorable downtown with a one-hundred-year-old drive-through creamery manned by smiley teens scooping out ice cream made from the milk of local cows. The town has at least six restaurants that have the word *bistro* in their name, including one called the Bistro. The most common annual income category here is "more than $200,000." In 2005 and 2007, Pleasanton was the wealthiest midsized city in the United States, and in 2014 *USA Today* ranked it the fourth best city to live in. Pleasanton is not a town for populists. Only 14.5 percent of the people in this county voted for Trump. These are not people interested in tearing down the elites. These are people interested in sitting in banquettes while eating traditional French home-style cooking.

I interviewed Scott over the phone in 1999, long before he went rogue, and he was even funnier and more self-deprecating than I'd expected. Like me, Scott is a coward, avoiding conflict in person but delighting in pissing people off through his writing. We have something even more unusual in common: we both don't believe in free will. We think decisions are unavoidable reactions of our physical brains to stimulus. In short, we are both really annoying.

We are also both members of the elite. In fact, Scott has more elite credentials than I do. He went to grad school at Berkeley, lives in the Bay Area, and co-founded a tech startup. He's paced stages with a PowerPoint clicker at elite events such as IBM Connect. He's a pescatarian. He's also more liberal on many social issues than I am. In addition to being an advocate for gay marriage, environmentalism, legalized marijuana, NFL quarterback Colin Kaepernick's right to kneel in protest for civil rights, and preventing men from deciding laws about abortion, he also thinks there should be a 25 percent income tax on the top 1 percent in order to provide African-Americans slavery reparations. He also believes he can self-actualize, which is five steps more Oprah than I will ever be. When preparing for the business-school entrance exam, he repeated, over and over, "I, Scott Adams, will score in the ninety-fourth percentile on my GMATs," which he accomplished. When he first peddled *Dilbert* to newspaper editors, he repeated, "I, Scott Adams, will become a syndicated cartoonist." Before his book *The Dilbert Principle* came out, his successful chant was "I, Scott

Adams, will be a number-one best seller." Scott is a guy I would not be surprised to run into at a party, especially if he had repeated "I, Scott Adams, will run into Joel Stein at a party."

But unlike everyone I meet at parties, Scott loves Donald Trump. Early in the presidential campaign, Scott began delivering nearly hourly Trump endorsements to his 270,000 Twitter followers. He still pens a *Dilbert* every day, but his passion is political commentary. He wrote a 2017 book called *Win Bigly: Persuasion in a World Where Facts Don't Matter* and appears on Fox News and CNN to rally for a populist revolution. Each morning, Scott logs onto Periscope, Twitter's video streaming service, where between 25,000 and 80,000 viewers watch him drink coffee in his home office as he calmly explains, often while drawing on a whiteboard, why Trump drained the swamp of yet more elite monsters. Kanye West has retweeted nine of his videos, Newt Gingrich mentioned one in a column, and Trump retweeted him during the campaign.

I'm not sure how to start a conversation with Scott that won't turn into an argument. I've got twenty minutes until our meeting, so I pull over to the side of the road to write down a few anodyne questions to get us started, when my phone pings with a text:

Okay to arrive early

I should not have downloaded that app.

＊　　＊　　＊

Scott greets me in his driveway, both because he is an excellent host and because he could see the precise second I was arriving. He is a short, bald, bespectacled sixty-one-year-old who is ripped in a way that makes me wonder if I grossly underestimated the physical effort involved in drawing cartoons. He looks like a man ready for the spittle-flying, high-speed debate style of populist cable news shows.

So I'm thrilled to find out that Scott is a sweet, smiley man who speaks slowly and softly. He's a terrific listener who squints a lot while you talk, as if he's making an effort to understand your point. There is nothing alpha about him. Other than his house.

You enter the Versailles of comic-strip royalty through a stone rotunda that leads to a huge-ceilinged open space that looks like a Napa winery. In addition to a pool, hot tub, sauna, gym, billiard room, and screening room, the 8,372-square-foot house contains rooms I have never seen in a home: an indoor tennis court, a massage room, a salon (pedicure chair, hair-washing sink, hair-cutting station), and a gift-wrapping room. There's a counter to hide a butler cart to transport drinks anywhere in the house. There are three microwaves (it's nice to reheat all your side dishes at once), two dishwashers (it's nice to load dirty dishes while cleaning others), washers and dryers both upstairs and downstairs (it's nice to take your clothes off anywhere), and a refrigerator full of nothing but half-pints of water (it's nice to not be thirsty). The huge backyard—landscaped with environmentally responsible fake grass—has a bocce ball court.

Scott and his wife designed this house for parties. Even though they divorced before it was built, he still threw ragers here. "A party in this house looked like the United Nations," he told me about his friends, a mix of people with ethnic backgrounds from Europe, South America, Africa, India, Japan, Mexico, and the Middle East. He hasn't thrown a party since the election. He doesn't go to any, either. His populism cost him about 75 percent of his friends. The gift-wrapping room has been repurposed as a place to play drums. The house feels lonely, like it wants drunk people running around naked, getting blowouts, pouring tiny bottles of water over each other's heads, and then fixing them with more blowouts. It feels like the Fourth of July at Benedict Arnold's.

As we stand in front of his screening room, Scott explains why his worldview and the elites' can no longer party together. He calls this theory "two movies on one screen." Sure, he and I are watching the same events. But due to cognitive dissonance (explaining away facts that contradict our worldview) and confirmation bias (remembering only the facts that support our worldview), he's shoveling popcorn into his mouth while laughing over a delightful comedy about a genius troll negotiating peace and prosperity. Meanwhile, I am gnawing on my nails while watching a horror film about an angry, incompetent racist with antisocial personality disorder destroying democratic norms. I very much want to see his movie. Because my movie sucks.

Scott informs me that I can indeed see his comedy. All I need is to choose to interpret events differently. Since cognitive dissonance and confirmation bias distort our lens no matter what we do, we should choose between messed-up lenses based on which does the best job of both making us happy and accurately predicting the future so we can make wise choices. Scott's lens caused him to predict Trump's victory, score a new career as a pundit, and watch a great movie.

Even though his friends think he bought a ticket to a snuff film, Scott doesn't feel like a traitor to his people. That's because he never felt like he was part of the elite. Not when he grew up in Windham, New York, a town not all that different from Miami, Texas, except it's smaller, whiter, older, and poorer. Not at Hartwick College, the school that Malcolm Gladwell argues in his book *David and Goliath* is better than Harvard if you're interested in the sciences since you're less likely to give up and switch majors. Not when he moved to California with nothing but $2,000 and two suitcases of belongings. Not when he got his MBA at Berkeley by going to night school because he worked during the day as a teller at a bank where he was robbed at gunpoint twice. If the CYRCLE artists knew about his struggle, they would have added more lines to their poster:

We left our families
We abandoned our homes
We had only two suitcases
We got robbed at gunpoint
Twice!

But when he succeeded as a cartoonist, Scott didn't enter the Loop. He's never met the editors at the newspapers that run *Dilbert*. He doesn't go to elite conferences. He doesn't even own a suit because he hasn't had an occasion to wear one. Scott was never given enough respect from the elite, who refuse to acknowledge the existence of any comic strip besides *Doonesbury*.

Dilbert is a salvo against elites. Its principal joke is that Dilbert's boss is a moron. People tacked *Dilbert* cartoons to their cubicles right where their bosses could see, like soldiers spray-painting an anarchist's red *A* on the side of their tanks. Surprisingly, their bosses didn't untack them. Instead, they taped *Dilbert* comics to the walls of their offices, mocking their own bosses. *Dilbert* wasn't a protest against middle management. It was a war cry against everyone in charge of everything. It's not only Dilbert's boss who is clueless, but also Dilbert's boss's boss. "It's turtles all the way up," Scott tells me. His book, *The Dilbert Principle*, explains his management theory, which is that companies promote the incompetent up the management chain to remove them from the workflow.

Bosses, Scott says, have no clue. This is the same argument Jerry used in Miami to convince me that the diplomats don't know how to deal with North Korea. It's the same rebel yell elite traitor Michael Gove (college at Oxford, editor at *The Times*; cabinet member) shouted to get people to vote for Brexit: "I think the people of this country have had enough of experts with organizations from acronyms saying that they know what is best and getting it consistently wrong." Normal, decent people hate acronyms, except when they're texting or trying to breathe underwater. Gisela Stuart, a member of Parliament who worked with Gove to pass Brexit, suggested the best method for weighing whether the UK should remain in a complex international economic and political union was this: "There is only one expert that matters, and that's you, the voter."

I ask Scott how many experts it took to build this house. He shows me a guest bathroom that has a corner where two cabinet drawers meet in a way that one can't be opened. This is what expert architects do. Besides, some of the ideas for his house came from more than 3,000 fans who sent ideas to the Dilbert's Ultimate House (DUH) project. These nonprofessionals are the ones responsible for the cat bathroom, the Christmas tree closet, and, most significantly, the enormous Dilbert head–shaped tower whose window-eyes overlook the pool. This is the Temple of Dilbert, a place to pray for the common man's victory over the elite. Except for these cabinet drawers. "There's no such thing as expertise. It just doesn't exist," Scott says. "The expert is full of shit." This seemed like an extreme opinion from a guy who got so good at hypnosis he has given women orgasms without touching them. Which are three things I have not mastered.

This is a major nihilistic escalation of Jerry's theory. It's not merely that experts get things wrong. Scott is saying that expertise is a scam. "Expertise is experience. One of the things I get from experience is seeing experts be wrong," he says. "What you perceive as Trump supporters' lack of sophistication is actually a superior sophistication. Because they see the number of times they've been conned." As part of his critique, Scott cites the replication crisis. A 2016 poll by *Nature* magazine found that 70 percent of scientists failed in their attempts to reproduce the results of an old experiment. Scott agrees that in my logical "2-D world" the scientific method would improve knowledge over time, squeezing out the false in favor of the true. But he says that in the actual "3-D world" we inhabit, all the scientists hang out and get blinded by mass delusion, thanks to cognitive dissonance and confirmation bias. In the 1970s, scientists falsely believed the population explosion would doom us. Now they might be wrong about global warming. "Make a list of all the things that science has said, throw a dart, and what are the odds of it being true?" he asks me. My list would include Bernoulli's principle, which allowed me to fly here; the Doppler effect, which allowed him to track me as I was driving here; and

$$\omega_0(\phi) = \frac{\cos\phi - \ell}{\sin\phi\sqrt{\frac{2}{\sin\phi}(1 - \ell\cos\phi - h\sin\phi)}}$$

which is the trajectory of a dart striking the center of a target.

Scott asks whether I would rather follow the nutritional advice of a hunter-gatherer or a government expert from the 1950s. Not only do I think this is cherry-picking a particularly bad historical moment for nutritional advice—why not make it a government expert smoking weed inside a candy factory—but I would indeed go with the Brylcreemed guy in the lab coat who told me to cook pork all the way through. I don't think hunter-gatherers had it all figured out as much as they didn't have a lot of options. I have no doubt that if they had a supermarket, hunters would have given their kids a diet of Ritz Crackers topped with Cheez Whiz, largely because Cheez Whiz doesn't attack you if you hit it with a spear. Actually, Cheez Whiz does, but in a far more entertaining way than a rhinoceros.

Scott doesn't even have faith in technological expertise despite the fact that he lives near Silicon Valley and knows a lot of engineers—including a fictional one he draws every day. "What did Steve Jobs know about making a computer? What did Apple know about making a smartphone? It's hard to think of any example in the corporate world where a person with more experience was replaced by a person with less experience and it was a disaster," he argues. He has been able to create tech products without an engineering education. In addition to the app that is still tracking me and probably will until the end of my days, Scott has a new app called Interface. According to its Silicon Valley–speak whitepaper, he created Interface "to deliver basic, blockchain-enabled video Interfacing." Specifically, it charges users to talk to experts. That's what Interface calls them: Experts. "Talk to an Expert, at any time, on any subject," the app advertises, though apparently an expert on capitalization is not yet available. This is the craziest thing I've learned about Scott yet, and he's got a washing machine both upstairs and downstairs.

As he shows me the app, I immediately laugh. Scott looks at me, confused. I look at him, confused about why he would be confused at a guy laughing at a guy who thinks experts are con artists and nevertheless is charging people to talk to them. He's pulling off a hilarious scam. Oh, Scott corrected me, he believes in certain forms of expertise: "On the small, yes. If I'm a gardener and my leaves are brown, I want to know, 'Why is that?'"

I see the entire plot of Scott's movie now. In the first act, an apprentice treks to a dojo in the middle of the snowy woods. In the second, he studies for decades with a sensei, reading old texts by candlelight at night. In the third act, he leaves on a dangerous mission to use his knowledge to revive browning leaves in a suburban backyard. Meanwhile, a crucial multinational trade deal that can deliver millions from poverty must be negotiated, so the sensei grabs a dude in a Starbucks mid-Frappuccino and has him do it.

Scott thinks this makes sense. He believes complexity doesn't require more expertise, but less. "In these big complicated situations, no one really knows if we have a good deal," he says. "It's best just to negotiate from ignorance and hope the other side gives in." Which sounds to me like playing poker without looking at your cards. Or knowing the rules of poker. "I bet there is no person who understands these deals. The cheese guy doesn't know the dairy guy, and the guy who negotiated it has moved on and things have shifted in the meantime. In the real world there is a fog. In a world where nobody knows, the loudest person is going to get the most," Scott says. This seems like arrogance, the equivalent of saying that if I don't understand quantum physics it doesn't exist. Or saying that if I don't know that cheese is a member of the dairy group, no one can. I'm sure Reid Hoffman knows the cheese guy, the dairy-other-than-cheese guy, and the negotiator guy, and they all get together for breakfast meetings.

This is the worldview Trump was advocating when

he tweeted, "Airplanes are becoming far too complex to fly. Pilots are no longer needed, but rather computer scientists from MIT. I see it all the time in many products. Always seeking to go one unnecessary step further, when often old and simpler is far better. Split second decisions are needed, and the complexity creates danger." He was pining for a period in aeronautics when passengers used barf bags and applauded when the landing didn't hurt. Advances such as collision avoidance systems have steadily lowered the number of fatal accidents per million flown miles on commercial planes by more than 93 percent since 1973.

Scott makes the same point as Trump when he says, "If you can figure out what the Fed does, or what it is, please tell me. I have no fucking idea." I could indeed tell him what the Fed does, which is largely raise or lower the federal funds rate to keep the economy at roughly 2 percent inflation in order to balance growth and price stability. My son, Laszlo, could tell him what the Fed does, because when he was six, he attended a free ninety-minute program for kids at the Federal Reserve in Richmond, Virginia. When it ended, the instructors gave him a bag of shredded money that he thought he could tape back together, and yet he still was able to understand what the Fed does.

I don't explain this to Scott because I have no doubt that he knows what the Fed does. He was an economics major in college and went to one of the best business schools in the country. But he denies that anything he learned was useful. "Economics is hardly anything. It's not a predictor of shit," he explains. In my movie script, ignoring basic economic rules predicts that you'll have shit on your hands. Literally. Populist leaders want to make people happy in the short term, so they lower interest rates to offer super-cheap loans, pretending this won't later cause runaway inflation. In Venezuela, this has led to a shortage of everything, including toilet paper, causing people to have to wipe with leaves. Unfortunately, Scott's anti-economist attitude is popular in the White House, where Peter Navarro, the director of the Office of Trade and Manufacturing Policy, said about working for Trump, "My function, really, as an economist is to try to provide the underlying analytics that confirm his intuition. And his intuition is always right in these matters."

Populism argues that the modern era requires ducking the barrage of facts because they are indistinguishable from lies. To walk right by the experts beckoning you to their three-card-monte game in which they shuffle graphs and statistics. "In your movie there's a big incompetent guy who doesn't know the details. I'm telling you it's the best thing possible. When President Trump acts without all the information and his facts are not accurate, he's operating on a higher level, not a lower level. He's operating in the real world. Lying misses the point that he's directionally true." This is the viewpoint that the philosopher Hannah Arendt, who escaped Nazi Germany after being imprisoned by the Gestapo for being Jewish, warned about. In 1951's *The Origins of Totalitarianism*, she wrote, "Instead of deserting leaders who had lied to them, they would protest they had all known all along the statement was a lie and admire the leaders for their superior tactical cleverness." Scott's argument that lies are good and truth is bad is the Orwellian core of authoritarianism. Arendt wrote, "The ideal subject of totalitarian rule is not the convinced Nazi or the convinced communist, but people for whom the distinction between fact and fiction…and the distinction between true and false…no longer exist."

I ask Scott how long he's had this belief in a complex system full of international dairy deals and basic, blockchain-enabled video interfacing that exists without expertise. "If I were eighteen years old and you asked me how often the best experts in the world were right, I would have said ninety-five percent of the time," he says. "If you asked me today, I'd say fifty-fifty."

When I was in elementary school, my family went to a cookout at my friend Joey Banker's house, where I believe I saw the adults smoke marijuana. I was the type of kid who was so uptight I thought rock and roll was the devil's music even though I was an atheist. So my parents' reefer madness was devastating. The world became fuzzy and large, and I remember staring at a sky filled with birds flying in indiscriminate patterns, one of which I thought was an eagle, possibly due to a contact high. It's the story I would tell over and over if someone had appointed me drug czar. But my epiphany wasn't about the dangers of gateway drugs. It was that my parents weren't perfect, and therefore adults weren't perfect, and therefore everyone in charge of everything wasn't perfect. Everything, I realized in that fake-eagle-soaring instant, is unsafe. No one should be trusted. I was alone. I went through sixth grade calling everyone in charge of anything a weasel. For the next decade I was sure anyone with any authority was in it for money or the Loop. I confused imperfection with complete corruption. I believed in the Meteorologist Fallacy™.

Scott's populist epiphany is a way better story than mine, despite its lack of drugs, eagles, rock and roll, or anything else that Sammy Hagar could use for lyrics. Scott's story of elitist disillusionment comes in three acts.

The first takes place in the 1990s when a Wells Fargo asset manager invested his savings in Enron, WorldCom, and Netscape. The first two of those companies tanked because of the management's deceitful accounting; Netscape went under because Microsoft violated antitrust law to destroy it. If that weren't enough to make Scott hate the elites, the entire field of stock picking has since proven to be an elitist con. Professional stock managers don't do better over time than throwing darts at a board of stocks without even knowing

$$\omega_0(\phi) = \frac{\cos\phi - \ell}{\sin\phi\sqrt{\frac{2}{\sin\phi}(1 - \ell\cos\phi - h\sin\phi)}}$$

Scott's second, far worse, experience with experts started with a spasm in his pinky finger.

CHAPTER 13

Care Actors

Eighteen months before I visited Scott, I was at a restaurant on vacation when my throat started to close. I'd put off seeing a doctor about my swollen glands for four months, and now I was suffering for it, unable to even swallow my own spit. On the flight home the next day I got a fever. I stayed in bed two days, although I didn't actually stay there for more than two hours at a time because I was constantly sprinting to the bathroom. Cassandra researched my symptoms online and figured out that I had a lymph abnormality that, hopefully, but not definitely, wasn't, though she couldn't be sure, cancer.

A doctor listened to Cassandra's diagnosis before telling me I'd gotten food poisoning in Mexico. Cassandra and the doctor got in a heated argument, as medical experts are apt to do. I tried to stop Cassandra so I could hear more from the doctor, whose diagnosis I respected due to her education, her experience, and the fact that linking explosive diarrhea to food from a tiny Mexican fishing village was something I should have figured out myself. Cassandra was furious at both the doctor and me, barely talking on the ride home. The experience made me worry that populism was causing health-care problems. Because that was easier than worrying that populism was causing marriage problems.

I spoke to a doctor who is one of the most prolific authors of WebMD articles after he assured me that he did not write "How Do You Handle a Scorpion Sting?" He told me he worries about his information being miscomprehended even though he tries to be clear and simple. Nevertheless, this doctor had patients angrily cite WebMD articles as evidence of their own misdiagnoses, and every so often this doctor got the pleasure of explaining that he wrote the article. When someone mentions an article I wrote, I never can tell if they misunderstood it because before they can say anything I interrupt them by yelling, "I wrote that!"

Kaiser Permanente, the largest private health-care provider in the United States, created a system to teach doctors how to handle difficult patients who contend that reading an article makes them more of an expert than they are. It's the same system we use to placate difficult people who think they're funnier than they are: improv.

Kaiser is a huge employer of part-time actors. These Care Actors have long performed in plays, including one for high-school audiences called *What Goes Around* that involves a character named Eli who cheats on his girlfriend and gets an STD, which he refers to as a "downtown souvenir." Care Actors also play irascible patients during improvisations with Kaiser doctors. I wanted to attend one of these sessions, partly so that when the improvisers asked the audience for a suggestion for a disease, I could yell "downtown souvenir!"

Kaiser, however, would not allow me to attend these sessions. So I set one up myself. I went on LinkedIn, looked for Kaiser Care Actors, and contacted Danielle Kennedy, a blonde-haired, blue-eyed actress who came to LA from Iowa in the 1960s and played the US ambassador on Netflix's *Narcos*. Danielle made it clear that she was not doing our bespoke session as a Care Actor, and that nothing she did or said represented Kaiser Permanente. By reading the rest of this chapter, you have legally agreed that you will forget that Danielle is a Care Actor as well as the entire idea of Care Actors, along with the words *acting* and *caring*, both of which I believe are trademarked by Kaiser Permanente.

Danielle and I met at the Encino Plaza Surgical Center to see my friend's husband, urologist Dr. Robert

Klein, who looks less like a real doctor than a TV doctor, with swooshy dark hair framing a handsome, boyish face. We got right into the improv, in which a hostile Danielle demanded bioidentical hormone replacement therapy. She said she read about its miraculous effects in Suzanne Somers's *The Sexy Years: Discover the Hormone Connection: The Secret to Fabulous Sex, Great Health, and Vitality, for Women and Men*, in which the author explains that the secret is to use a lot of colons and subheads. Dr. Klein listened patiently and then said, "She's so full of shit it's unbelievable." This annoyed Danielle, who liked Suzanne Somers and hated that menopause has caused her to "get irritable," "sweat like crazy," and "be dry." None of this was covered in high-school sex-ed class, which spent way too much time on the fallopian tubes, which have never since come up other than the time I foolishly whispered in a woman's ear, "Can you feel that in your fallopian tubes?"

I would give a sweaty menopausal woman whatever she wanted. But Dr. Klein kept his cool. When Danielle irritably and drily repeated her demand for a prescription, Dr. Klein blew her off by saying "I can write you a prescription for anything. I got a license. Let's go party." As a fan of improv, I thought Danielle would "yes, and…" him and they'd pretend to go to an electronic music festival, trip on molly, have sex, and get a downtown souvenir. But instead, she continued demanding the prescription. Dr. Klein got very rational, explaining the increased risk percentage of heart attacks that is a side effect of bioidentical hormones. He got Danielle to agree to start with a hormone panel test to see if there were other reasons for her distemper. "Maybe your husband is a pain in the ass and driving you crazy," he said. This seemed to be a good guess because Danielle said that he reacted to her lack of sex drive by asking, "What the hell is wrong with you all of the sudden?" This seemed even less sexy than my fallopian tubes line.

When they finished, I clapped and asked Danielle how Dr. Klein performed. Her only critique was that he made jokes at moments when she wanted to be taken seriously—precisely the cockiness that makes us hate experts. It's the smug IT guy standing over your computer, lording his nerddom over you. It's McKinsey & Company consultants suggesting you fire workers whose jobs they don't understand. For me, it's the auto mechanic spouting obscure jargon such as "transmission" and "tires." But being dismissive is an effective way to exert your expertise when it's doubted. Danielle admitted that Dr. Klein's confidence helped convince her of his diagnosis. Most of the time Danielle has to steer doctors the other way, helping ones who are young or new to our country avoid getting bullied into treatments they don't believe in, which is a bigger concern for Kaiser. But being harsh is also a problem because bedside manner is the main way people choose doctors. Dr. Klein said he inoculates himself against patient anger by warning them that doctors aren't always right. Patients with obscure diseases often know more than he does. As do those with problems outside of his expertise. He doesn't want to return to an era in which doctors were held in such esteem that patients were too embarrassed to reveal important information, which is the second-best euphemism I've heard for a venereal disease after "downtown souvenir."

Scott Adams was one of those patients whose medical problems were outside of his doctor's purview. In 2003, he started getting spasms in his pinky so intense that he couldn't draw straight lines. He produced *Dilbert* with a digital stylus, which required a lighter touch that allowed him to draw. Two years later, he lost his voice. He could sing, recite poetry, and force out sentences while pinching his nose, but human conversation was a gasp-y, stammering ordeal. Scott could give an hour-long speech to an audience or talk on-camera, but was muted at parties. Doctors failed to find diseases or polyps, so they sent him to a psychologist, who prescribed him Valium for stress. Even if, like Scott, you don't believe in free will, it's still humiliating and frustrating to be told your problem is in your head when you're sure it isn't. Instead of taking the Valium, he slowly repeated this affirmation over and over: "I, Scott, will speak perfectly." Which, ironically, is the kind of thing a person would do on Valium.

Not talking provides you with lots of free time, which is another thing you can get from taking Valium. Scott used his to research his problem online, discovering that his pinky spasms and voice loss were both symptoms of spasmodic dysphonia. None of the doctors had mentioned this disease to him, despite all their expertise, which, apparently, did not include how to perform an Internet search. He found a specialist who confirmed his diagnosis and prescribed Botox shots through his neck into his voice box, which didn't work that well but made his voice box look ten years younger. In 2008, his continuing research led him to Gerald Berke, the chief of UCLA Medical Center's Division of Head and Neck Surgery, who had developed an operation in which he snips a nerve near the larynx and replaces it with another one from the body. Scott was completely cured.

"Who said it couldn't be fixed? Doctors. Who said it could? Me," Scott says. The way I see it, Scott was saved by a medical field so packed with expertise it cured a disease so obscure only about 50,000 people have it. It's not as if Scott grabbed a knife himself and replaced a nerve in his throat. I don't even think Scott could draw someone doing that. The person who said it could be fixed was a surgeon who was the chief of UCLA Medical Center's Division of Head and Neck Surgery and a former president of the Triological Society, the main academic society in otolaryngology. It's like saying that no one understood your physics problem until you solved it yourself by going to Princeton to ask Albert Einstein. If this is Scott's reason for hating the elite, it's a faulty one. Condemning all experts based on the failure of a few to solve a very difficult problem is the Meteorologist Fallacy™.

The weirdest thing about the Meteorologist Fallacy™ is that no one truly believes in it. You might complain that the medical field is corrupt, but when you need an operation, you walk over to the doctor's wall and examine those diplomas. People who complain that the weather report is useless still consult the weather report. The Meteorologist Fallacy™ is one of those dangerous worldviews that we apply to others but not ourselves.

Still, I understand Scott's frustration. I got chiggers from orienteering in the woods in Tennessee and my Beverly Hills doctor, unfamiliar with orienteering, Tennessee, or woods, thought it was a rash and gave me a shot of steroids. The steroid shot did nothing other than melding the chigger DNA with my own DNA and turning me into Chiggerman, a superhero who doesn't get to fight crime because he has to spend all his time calming African-American citizens who misheard him when he announced his superhero name.

Scott judges the doctors who dismissed his symptoms as elites who were less interested in helping others than in maintaining their status. They're corrupt, having been captured by a drug company or a government agency. "Anyone who can get away with something, if there's a high payoff and a low chance of getting caught, they're doing it," Scott says, handing me a refrigerated tiny bottle of water, which I accept even though we elites prefer room-temperature water. "For every politician with a lot of power, there's a billionaire behind him. It's *Game of Thrones* with billionaires." The idea that America is corrupt is so widely accepted it's challenging to explain how wrong it is. In 2015, we were the sixteenth least corrupt out of 176 countries. Yet in that year 75 percent of Americans said corruption in our government was "widespread." Incorrectly believing that corruption is rampant leads people to shrug off actual corruption as the norm, thus allowing it to proliferate. This myth of mass corruption will lead us to eventually become one of the 100 most corrupt countries, where the government acts like the mafia, requiring you to pay off cops, bribe inspectors, and accept money that was obviously once shredded and then taped together by a six-year-old boy.

The mistaken assumption that corruption is ubiquitous led Trump to consider commuting the jail term of Rod Blagojevich. The former Democratic Illinois governor was really into corruption. He told a children's hospital their funding would be cut off if their CEO didn't contribute $50,000 to his campaign. He tried to sell the Senate seat vacated by Barack Obama that he was in charge of filling. The FBI recorded Blagojevich saying, "It's a fucking valuable thing. You just don't give it away for nothing." Trump believes this is no big deal, since selling appointments is something he's sure elected officials do all the time. It is not, thanks to the hard-fought late-nineteenth-century civil service reforms that politicians such as Theodore Roosevelt made a priority, at the cost of nearly splitting the Republican Party. But Trump thought that Blagojevich, even though he's a member of the opposing party, was treated unfairly. "Plenty of other politicians have said a lot worse," Trump said about the FBI tapes. Acting jaded about corruption and lying seems brave, authentic, and worldly, but it's merely the lie kids tell to justify insane demands. It's the "all the other kids eat sugar cereals" of debate tactics.

Scott and I stroll down Pleasanton's idyllic Main Street to have lunch at Pastas Trattoria, which is Italian for "Pastas Bistro." The restaurant is playing one of my favorite country songs, Eric Church's "Round Here Buzz." It's surreal to hear Church pine over an ex-girlfriend who foolishly abandoned his tiny Texan town for the elite folderol of the city while eating in this Pleasanton trattoria that serves a Snake River Farms Wagyu burger. The restaurant should be playing a song from the ex-girlfriend's side instead:

We left our families
We abandoned our homes

We worked for nothing
We slept on floors
We ate this amazing Wagyu burger!

Pastas Trattoria then plays John Denver's "Take Me Home, Country Roads." The new American myth that authenticity requires remaining in your hometown has crept all the way to Pleasanton, where more than a quarter of the citizens were born in a different country. Then again, the songwriters who pined for country roads to take them back to the place they belonged, West Virginia, were a Massachusettsian and a Washingtonian who had never been to West Virginia. Eric Church lives in Nashville, Tennessee, not the 1,200-person town of Blowing Rock, North Carolina, where he grew up. They're all populist elites.

As I listen to the music, I swipe a slice of bread through a plate of balsamic vinegar floating on a pool of olive oil and try to figure out how to ask Scott an indelicate question. One that might explain Scott's populist turn. One that I hope doesn't end our talk.

CHAPTER 14

A Meme Guy

K ristina Basham is a twenty-nine-year-old model with 4.5 million Instagram followers largely based on her bikini photos. That is an assumption on my part. It might be due to her posts of inspirational quotes such as "Stay close to people who feel like sunlight" and "I'm looking for a moisturizer that hides the fact that I've been tired since 2012." But I'm guessing it's the photos, since *BroBible*, which is the bible for bros, featured her in their "daily sexy Instagram roundup" several times, whereas the *Paris Review* hasn't run her poetry even once. According to her Instagram bio, Kristina plays violin and piano, is a "skincare guru," and wants people to know that "I like to smile, smiling's my favorite ☺".

Scott Adams lives down the street from Kristina. He needed a model for his book, and being a nice guy who didn't want to ask someone to smile who wasn't really into it, asked her to pose for him. Though the photos never made it into the book, they started dating. Not long after, Kristina moved into his house. Where, to Scott's great fortune, she never opened his book to see if there were photos in it.

A bikini-model girlfriend isn't the main data point that makes me want to ruin Scott's meal and ask if he's having a midlife crisis. Neither is the fact that he posted shirtless photos of his six-pack abs on Twitter. Or that he's got a man cave. Or started playing drums. It's that his embrace of populism seems like buying a sports car. It's living in the moment, embracing risk, unshackling from polite society. Supporting Trump is a line of political cocaine.

It's also a shot of testosterone. Populism is a primal scream for primordial masculinity. It's a call for action over thought, individualism over cooperation. It's un-controlled emotion: fighting, insulting, bragging, sleeping around, and bragging about the attractiveness of your wife even though you're also sleeping around. It's everything the eggheads in salmon pants are not. Scott told me that the Democratic Party is symbol-ically female and committed to finding fairness. Re-publicans are metaphorically male and understand that fairness is both impossible and disincentivizing, so in-stead of justice they aim for power. On the last day of the 2016 Democratic National Convention, Scott tweeted: "Did the Democratic convention make you feel like a weak and useless white male? That's why I didn't watch."

I lower my head both to avoid eye contact and reveal my thinning hair. "Is it possible you're having a midlife crisis?" I ask.

Scott is not a man offended by questions. It's a big part of his charm. He's interested in difficult discussions. Scott says that he might be having a midlife crisis, but it's not what brought him to his political convictions. It's that his old movie wasn't as good as his new one.

As he explains the plot of his movie about Trump, it starts to seem less foreign to me. In it, a scrappy trickster takes on the uptight powers that be. That's a movie I love. I hate the uptight powers that be. The smug, mannered class and their tiny problems caused me to hate *Pride and Prejudice* in high school. I winced at a cappella groups in college even before I learned the incomprehensible fact that women find them attractive. Making fun of authority was my raison d'être, a phrase I loved making fun of. On a trip to DC in high school to a Junior State of America convention, I disrupted the mock election between George H. W. Bush and Michael Dukakis with a third-party campaign for David Letterman. I arranged the letters on the sign in our high-school lobby to quote Paul Simon: "When I think back on all the crap I learned in high school, it's a wonder I can think at all." When I interviewed Scott for *Time* in 1999, one of my questions was "If you wanted, you could draw better than that, right?" I used to be a real dick.

At our Stanford orientation the entire incoming class listened to a speech from co–student president Ingrid Nava, who berated us for ignoring the plight of Latino gardeners working on campus. I was pretty sure I wasn't responsible for these inequities because I had been a member of the elite for only three days. I later wrote an extremely offensive column for the *Stanford Daily* that, luckily, the editor yanked from the paper. I wrote it from Ingrid Nava's perspective, donning a Carmen Miranda fruit hat in my photo and beginning with "Hate. Hate. Hate. Anger. Anger. Anger. Salsa. Salsa. Salsa." I am glad I no longer insult ethnic groups in print and transgender people in photos, but I miss taking on whatever establishment is put in front of me.

"You and I have a similar brand. We mock the elite. That's part of our job," Scott said. "The amount of fun Trump supporters have is huge. You think you're having one conversation but one side is laughing and one is crying. The memes are great. I have a meme guy. Some are too mean so I don't put my name on the memes." Mean memes do sound fun. When people point out typos in his blog posts, Scott leaves them in to troll the finger-waving grammar elitists. Trump's staff members go one step farther and purposely insert grammatical errors when they tweet for him because it twists up the elite. Who doesn't love making grammarians angry by breaking every prissy, can't-end-a-sentence-with-a-preposition rule you can think of? This is not how my stuffy elite friends think. My college friend Martha Brockenbrough, who wrote an anti-Trump children's book called *Unpresidented*, founded the Society for the Promotion of Good Grammar. Someone else I know has a T-shirt that says I'M SILENTLY CORRECTING YOUR GRAMMAR. Maybe I am watching the wrong movie merely because it's the only one playing in my self-serious neighborhood.

"You would love this side," Scott says to me.

He says this in a nice way, with no belabored breaths through a black mask, but it still makes me dislike his movie. It might be more exciting than mine, but it's got a way bigger chance of ending with the destruction of a planet. I have become conservative in the truest sense, advocating for small incremental improvements and against attacking the system now that I've seen places that don't have a system. I have lost my punk. I'd never ask Scott if he could draw better now. I'd never write that self-aggrieved, salsa-salsa-salsa column now because I've learned to control my MRI-diagnosed racism. I've tamped down the instinctual fear that people in Miami, Texas, expressed about another group gaining power.

As a tween I often giggled uncontrollably. So much was foreign and improbable: death, dismemberment,

the word *pussyfooting* that I still believe the vice principal of my middle school baited me with when asking
why I was late to the cafeteria. Those things now seem
real. People I love have died. I've known people who
got dismembered. And, thanks to the Internet, I've seen
women pussyfooted. The world seems fragile and I
want trustworthy, trained people running it. I want that
more than I want it run by people who share my values
or act like me. I want that more than I want to be funny.
I want that more than I want great memes.

Walking down Main Street after lunch, Scott gets a
call from a producer at Fox News. People from Fox
call often, since he has a knack for delivering the most
provocative take on that day's news in his morning
coffee lectures. A month after our lunch, he'll buy a
suit at Men's Wearhouse for a meeting with President
Trump in the Oval Office. "I'm the most successful
political commentator in the last two years," he says
after finishing the Fox News call, "without any experience." This was the third act in Scott's elitist disillusionment. The pundits, pollsters, and politicians were
wrong about the election and he was right. "From
when I was young, I thought I would be an influential
person in the world, simply by being a reasonable person. That would be rare and valued," Scott says. It's
the populist version of a children's fairy tale: He was
chosen not because he had the DNA of wizards but
because he was average. Innate reasonableness is his
superpower. And superheroes don't need training.

I wonder how much Scott believes in his own political skills. How much does he believe that expertise is unnecessary?

"Could you be secretary of state?" I ask.

Absolutely not, he tells me.

I am greatly relieved. We at least agree that someone who only recently ventured outside the country for the first time, is disinterested in foreign policy, and spent his career drawing funny pictures shouldn't be the most powerful nation's top emissary. Then Scott adds, "I lack the memory and stamina."

On my list of why the *Dilbert* guy shouldn't be secretary of state, "memory" and "stamina" would be 234th and 235th. But they're number one and two for Scott. Number three is: "And I wouldn't like it. If you could imagine me in some job where you don't have to memorize a bunch of world leaders' names and travel around the world? Yes." I fear we are a few years away from the Senate confirmation hearing for secretary of state consisting solely of the question, "Dude, you afraid of flying?" I ask Scott if he could effectively serve as secretary of education or housing and urban development. "Yes," he answers. "Probably yes."

A 2010 study found that 30 percent of college students had narcissistic personality traits, which is 50 percent more than in the early 1980s. The most common dream job in my son's first-grade class wasn't doctor or firefighter, it was YouTuber, which is an especially lame dream since it's something they could have done right then. It's not because I live in LA, either; it was true for my nephew's first-grade class in New Jersey. It's not only young people: my mom's email signature is "To thine own self be true," which is Shakespearean for "Fuck everyone else." Once you consider yourself a special person, it's a small step to believe you're special at everything. We confidently boast to our TV screens that we could have made a better decision than the coach of an NFL team or the president of the United States. This is not at all true. Since 2000, during each party's first presidential debate, I try to calculate if I would do a better job than anyone onstage. Of the sixty-five candidates, I've guessed I could govern better than four of them, and only one of those four became president.

People's overestimation of their abilities has been compounded by the fact that technology reduced barriers to entry. On a screen, a blogger's thoughts on Middle East affairs look similar to a *New York Times* column written by a member of the Council on Foreign Relations. The punditry Scott broadcasts from his phone looks the same as analysis from a former White House employee on CNN. In an astonishing display of hubris, a lot of people post homemade pornography. I cannot imagine how confident you have to be to assume strangers want to see you have sex. I know that no one wants to see me having sex. Not even Cassandra, based on how quickly she turns out the lights.

Narcissism has been destroying truth. Liberals have

been dangerously eroding the word *truth* when they use it instead of *perspective* or *side of the story* in the phrase "sharing your truth." On college campuses, believing in science itself is questioned because it has been used by those in power to oppress others: phrenology to justify racism, nutrition to shame fat people, and psychology to institutionalize gays. In its place, professors teach truths based on personal narratives that can't be questioned by people outside the author's tribe because they cannot know the truth of that group's experience. Scott's two-movies theory is the reigning philosophic outlook. It was originally called perspectivism by Friedrich Nietzsche and it states that due to the limits of our dumb brains, we can only see from our point of view and not from an objective position, so truth is unknowable in a practical sense. Everything is equally true and false. Every fact is a cat in Schrödinger's box. Or as Scott writes in his book, in an aphorism Nietzsche would admire: "Facts don't matter. What matters is how you feel."

That idea has smashed truth into enough snowflake-shaped shards for everyone to have their own. I know how easy it is to sledgehammer truth. Not because I've watched it nearly destroy journalism. Because I've met the people gleefully doing the demolition.

CHAPTER 15

Littering on the
Death Star

I know it's him right away. That's because he's the
only one in the restaurant. Otherwise, I would
never have guessed this guy is a fake news kingpin. He's not wearing a shiny suit or tight jeans or a
T-shirt that says FAKE NEWS KINGPIN. He's a short,
bald, white guy about my age, smiling and waving
at me from the banquette at this Orange County
seafood restaurant. He's wearing a button-down shirt
and khakis, looking less like an evil mastermind than a
Dilbert character. This is not how I pictured the guy
who got Fox News to repeat a false story he made up
about Obama using his own money to keep a Muslim
museum open during a government shutdown. And
who fabricated an article titled "The Assam Rape Festival in India Begins This Week" that caused India's

cybercrimes unit to launch an investigation. And who wrote "FBI Agent Suspected in Hillary Email Leaks Found Dead in Apparent Murder-Suicide," which was seen by 1.6 million people right before the presidential election.

Jestin Coler is a general in the war against truth, blasting a hole in people's trust in the press. Which is deeply troublesome because the press is democracy's greatest weapon against autocracy, other than voting. And legislatures. And courts. And the military's allegiance to the Constitution over the commander in chief. And maybe America's rebellious, independent DNA. But still, the press is high enough on the list that it's usually the first industry dictators take over. I have come here to find out why someone would put democracy at risk. Did he do it because he's a white supremacist? An isolationist? And if he tells me the reason he did it, how can I be sure, given his background, that he isn't lying?

Jestin is nothing like the other fast-talking conspiracy-theorist alt-right provocateurs I've met. He's humble and shy. He's got the unassuming demeanor of someone who grew up in Angola, Indiana, a rural town with fewer than 9,000 people, 93.6 percent of whom are white—half a percentage lower than Miami's. Still, as nice as he seems, I brace myself for Jestin's attack on liberal elites.

But Jestin says he voted for Hillary Clinton. Even in the primary against Bernie Sanders. This is surprising considering that he started a successful propaganda campaign against Hillary Clinton.

He didn't mean to. The reason Jestin looks and acts like one of my liberal friends in the media is that Jestin was a liberal member of the media. He even grew up liberal. While his neighbors were conservative and religious, Jestin's parents were liberals who didn't take him to church. He was the snowflake in town, like Susan Bowers at the Rafter B Café in Miami. Like any elite, Jestin left Angola immediately after graduating high school, packing his stuff in a van and driving south until he hit a major city, just like the CYRCLE poster advised. After putting himself through college by working at a Barnes & Noble, he landed a job working for a group of magazines in Fort Lauderdale. He wasn't paid well but loved being in the Loop, covering parties and writing movie reviews. When print advertising collapsed, the company laid him off and he got a job managing databases in suburban Southern California, mostly working from his home. Already a news junkie and torn away from an office of fellow journalists, Jestin spent much of his day reading news websites and getting incensed about the stupidity of the alt-right. One night, he came up with a plan to catfish them. He wrote a fake news story claiming that one of their hateful, addle-brained conspiracy theories was true. Then he waited for the alt-right to believe it. At which point he would reveal his article was fake, thereby exposing their stupidity and destroying their movement. The first half of his plan worked. His fake news story got lots of views from conservatives who thought it was true. But no one cared when he revealed it was fake. People felt it was directionally true. Even if these particulars didn't happen on this particular occasion, something very much like it was probably happening somewhere. Facts didn't matter. What mattered was how his article made them feel. More surprising was that the success of his trap made its existence less believable. How could something be completely false if so many people shared it? It had been verified by the masses. The Chinese saying for this is "Three men make a tiger," which states that if enough people make up a story about a tiger hanging out at a busy market, everyone will believe it. In other words, all I need is two more people to claim this Chinese phrase was turned into an awful movie in which Tom Selleck, Ted Danson, and Steve Guttenberg adopt an adorable baby tiger that claws them to death.

Whereas Jestin had been making a dollar a word writing real journalism, he could sell $10,000 in ads for a successful 500-word fake article. As soon as he found this out, Jestin switched his goal from political-science experiment to making-money experiment. Besides, his dream had been writing parodies for *The Onion*. Now he was doing that, only some people were too dumb to get the jokes. He created websites with legit-sounding names such as DenverGuardian.com and Washington-Post.com.co and filled them with pro-Trump fiction.

Jestin didn't need any Soviet-level disinformation training. Truth had become flimsy enough that he could flip it like an egg. "People think fake news has damaged the credibility of journalists. I think it's the other way around. They've been not talking to the people for so long it gave rise to others who could. If you don't see stories that are relevant to yourself on the *Washington Post,* you might wind up on Breitbart," he said. Or WashingtonPost.com.co. Jestin agues that because the elites didn't come to Miami, Texas, the townsfolk listened to the snake-oil salesman who did.

When Jerry Wilmoth told me on the porch that he stopped reading *Time* because it's too liberal, I figured I was about to hear a rant about how Fox News was fair. That is not what Jerry believed. He believed Fox News is a wing of the Republican Party. This was a great relief until he added that CNN and the *New York Times* are wings of the Democratic Party. All news, he believed, is propaganda. This is a hard argument to combat because *Time,* the *New York Times,* and CNN are indeed staffed nearly entirely by liberals; I watched reporters cry in the *Time* offices when the Bush v. Gore verdict came in. This is not new: the conservative founder of *Time,* Henry Luce, grumbled about his staff, "For some goddamn reason, Republicans can't write." But I also know that editors and executives I've worked for don't collude with Democratic Party leaders the same way those at Fox News do with the GOP. I know that the *New York Times* fidelity is to truth, not policy.

I also know that people think I'm lying about this. The percent of Americans who have a "great deal of confidence in the press" was down to 8 percent in 2016; it had been 28 percent in 1976. Rush Limbaugh declared the Four Corners of Deceit to be government, academia, science, and media. Sure, there's a logic flaw in being told not to trust the media by one of the most influential members of the media, but nerdily pointing out logical fallacies is exactly the kind of sneaky lawyer crap the media pulls. In 2017, Pew found that 85 percent of Republicans say the news media has "a negative effect on the way things are going in this country." It's not only conservatives who feel this way. More Democrats agreed with that statement than disagreed. When I was talking to Mayor Eric Garcetti about how people faulted his practical, pothole-fixing style of governing for not being ambitious enough, he said, "It was really unsatisfying to the elites like the *LA Times* editorial board and the mucky-mucks to have a mayor doing what a mayor is supposed to do." Hating the media is so acceptable that he said this to me even though he knew I had worked for the *LA Times* op-ed section.

It's not merely trust in media that has evaporated. In 1964, 77 percent of Americans said they trusted the government in Washington, and by 2011 only 17 percent did. In 1975, 44 percent of Americans said they had "a great deal" of confidence in "the church or organized religion," but by 2018 only 20 percent did. In 1993, Sting sang "If I Ever Lose My Faith in You." It is not a political song. It's a love song you hear in dentists' offices. It also didn't come out during a dark time for the Western world. In 1993, the elites were killing it: the European Union was created and the North American Free Trade Agreement was signed. The album this song is on, *Ten Summoner's Tales*, is meant to appeal to the elite: it is named after Chaucer's *The Canterbury Tales* and was recorded at Sting's 1578 Elizabethan country house. Yet in the song, Sting proclaims he has lost his faith in science, progress, the church, television media, and all politicians. Sting even lost his faith in nonfiction books, which I know because he did not grant me the rights to quote his song. Trusting nothing was already so ingrained in late-twentieth-century culture that Sting was using it as the piffle you throw out to get laid, the modern equivalent of "Baby, it's cold outside."

When you distrust elites it seeps into everything. Back in 1960, 58 percent of Americans believed "most people can be trusted." In 2014, that number had dropped by nearly half. When people don't gather in person to grind out differences at their church groups, town councils, and Odd Fellows embalmings, they stew in their houses, ascribing bad motives to those who disagree with them. Once you suspect everyone else is a selfish liar, it's hard for a society to function. When you have no trust in institutions, you don't believe that mom or dad can settle an argument. So you have to fight to the death.

Trust has also been decimated by digital information. Humans are living by rules built for computers, which can instantly digest oceans of data. Our brains cannot. The Internet is the opposite of novels: it's an empathy-reducing machine. In 1894, Leo Tolstoy already saw that the modern world's barrage of information would decay trust. In his treatise on Christian nonviolence, *The Kingdom of God Is Within You*, he wrote:

> The more men are freed from privation; the more telegraphs, telephones, books, papers, and journals there are; the more means there will be of diffusing inconsistent lies and hypocrisies, and the more disunited and consequently miserable will men become.

There's so little trust that people didn't even believe Jestin's articles. Or maybe they did. There's no way to know, since they didn't even read them. They saw the headlines on Facebook and forwarded them to others. Rarely did they click on the link to the article, and when they did, they almost never got past the third paragraph. Jestin tested this repeatedly by throwing sentences into the end of the article that strongly hinted the articles were fake, such as "This article is fake."

Articles are no longer consumed to learn facts.

Articles are grenades to throw at your enemies. It's not that foreign governments, unscrupulous politicians, or greedy media companies are pushing propaganda. We're all doing it. In his 1970 book, *Culture Is Our Business*, Marshall McLuhan predicted: "World War III is a guerrilla information war with no division between military and civilian participation." The most famous fake news website, run by conspiracy theorist Alex Jones, is called InfoWars.

Writing fake news was so easy that Jestin often did it drunk. He said I could do it, too, no problem. I couldn't believe this was true. So I had a few drinks, wrote this, and sent it to Jestin for his appraisal:

Black Lives Matter: Oakland Strips Police of Their Guns

Oakland, California—In a five-to-three vote on Monday, the Oakland City Council passed legislation written by Black Lives Matter activists that bans officers from carrying guns. SWAT team members will be allowed to bring non-automatic weapons on a case-by-case basis.

Mayor Libby Schaaf compared the current police force to a "frat house" with a "culture of toxic masculinity." At a community meeting announcing the plan, she said, "If an officer can't resolve a situation by using her or his words, then she or he isn't a good enough officer for the Oakland Police Department."

The law is scheduled to go into effect on January 16, which is Martin Luther King Jr. Day. Black Lives Matter activists plan to celebrate with looting and gangster rapping.

Jestin praised it as "subtle." I was horrified that there's a part of media so vile that my writing could be considered subtle.

Shortly after the election, NPR reporters knocked on Jestin's door, having traced the fake news websites to him. His anonymity was hurt by the fact that he called his company DisInfoMedia. It also didn't help that his parents gave him a name with the word *jest* in it. Jestin was blamed for Clinton's loss. He was lambasted on *60 Minutes* and received death threats. He left the fake news business.

But the fake news business hasn't left us. A fake news story landed in my Twitter account after being retweeted by MSNBC host Lawrence O'Donnell. Text had been seamlessly inserted into a screenshot of *In Touch Weekly* magazine's interview with the porn star Stormy Daniels about her tryst with Trump. The fake additions to her quotes read:

We ended up having dinner in the room. I'll never forget his order. He calls up room service and goes,

"I want a pizza and I want the toppings on the pizza to be littler pizzas. Like the size of pepperonis but they're actually full pizzas, just little." So then he hangs up and I assume he's going to make his move on me but instead he gets up, and in this really sing-songy voice starts going, "I'm having pizaaaas, with little pizzaaaas on top, I'm having pizaaaas, with little pizzaaaas on top." Then he goes, "I'm going to give you the night of your life. I'm going to f—— you so hard your p—— is going to feel like it just ate a pizza with tiny pizzas as the topping." He was trying to sell me I guess.

It was posted by Justin Halpern, whose name is like Jestin's except normal. Justin is a sitcom writer who is the author of the best-selling book *Sh*t My Dad Says*. He clearly wasn't doing it for money. He also had no motive to catfish liberals because he is a liberal. Justin has been a member of the liberal elite from birth. The dad he mocked in his book is a retired doctor of nuclear medicine in San Diego. Why would someone like that slap away our fingernail hold on truth?

Like Jestin, Justin got in the fake news game accidentally. He assumed everyone would know it was parody when he doctored a *New York Times* article to claim that Paul Ryan blasted a Papa Roach song about suicide from his SUV after his bill repealing Obamacare was defeated. "I thought liberals were less likely to fall for this," he said. But cognitive dissonance sees no political affiliation. "There's no safe harbor. Just a bunch of people who think, 'Yeah, this makes this guy look like shit. Let's just believe it,'" he said.

Fake news has become even easier to create than when Jestin pumped stuff out. Justin explained how he does it: You can go to a real news website, click on Google Chrome's inspect feature, replace any words you like, and see the perfect doctored version on your screen. Then you take a screenshot and post it on social media. "It shouldn't be legal," Justin said. That's because it is not at all legal, according to copyright law.

I used Google Chrome's inspect feature with the same article about Stormy Daniels to see if it was as easy as Justin said. In ten minutes, I had inserted my own sentences into her quotes:

> We hung out for a while. He turned on Fox News and they were interviewing some senator. And he's like, "I'm smarter than all fifty senators." And I was like, "Um, there are a hundred senators." And he was like, "No, honeybunch, fifty." Then he started singing that song, you know, about how there are fifty nifty states. The kids' song. "Fifty nifty, United States, from thirteen original colonies." I try to explain that each state has two senators, but he won't stop singing. He got through the whole song. He was very proud of himself, like he was trying to impress me or something.

No one would believe this, I thought. To make sure, I posted it on Twitter. Almost immediately, Justin Diedrich, a "progressive gynecologist from Southern California," retweeted my fake news article. He wrote how great it was that "Trump sang that kids' song!" I couldn't believe how easy it was to fool someone. A liberal someone who went to medical school.

I felt upset, and only partially because I knew how confusing it was going to be to quote another person named Justin in this chapter. I wrote to Dr. Justin to confess I made the story up. Then I called him to apologize, which, according to his terms, required singing the entire "Fifty Nifty United States" song to him. Dr. Justin told me he was less disappointed about being tricked by a journalist than about the fact that my story wasn't true. "I pictured Trump breaking out into song and it was such a great image in my head that I latched onto it," he told me. "It's elitist of us to think we're not as susceptible as liberals to things that back up what we believe. It's confirmation bias."

When Clinton was expected to win, Jestin Coler tried putting out anti-Trump fake news articles, but almost no one clicked on them. "My working assumption at the time was that conservatives will fall for anything. They were less educated, more religious," Jestin says. "What I think now is that it has to do with your position. Fake news has shifted to where you can get liberals to fall for something because they want to hear things. It's a change in the balance of power."

Being disempowered is the fuel for conspiracy theories. It's the fuel for impeachment talk at Stephanie Miller Resistance Dinner Parties.

Justin the sitcom writer still puts out fake news stories, even though he knows a lot of people are going to believe them. "The ultimate peace I made with this was that it says more about the problems with democracy than I could ever write. I'm littering on the Death Star as it's exploding," he said. Even Jestin Coler doesn't feel as badly as people want him to. "I sold a little bit of my soul and made a lot of money. I didn't do anything illegal. Is what I did unethical? Yes. But I didn't hurt anyone," he says.

But by changing the norms so much that lying has been crossed off the Ten Commandments—which I can do using Google Chrome's inspect feature—we have indeed hurt people. An inability to know what's true leads to two movies, which leads to battle. On a 1968 Canadian TV show, Marshall McLuhan said, "When you give people too much information, they instantly revert to pattern recognition." This simplification, he argued, would lead to cardboard-cutout stereotypes of others. "An electronic world retribalizes man," he said.

Scott Adams showed me exactly how this retribalization works, right on his computer.

CHAPTER 16

Son of Fidel Castro

A re you serious? Are you fucking serious?"
Scott asks me, shaking his head. "Oh my lord.
The things you don't see."

I am confused. He had called me a liberal and compared me to "Justin Trudeau, the son of Fidel Castro." I laughed, thinking that "son of Fidel Castro" is a hyperbolic way of describing the Canadian prime minister's politics. But from the way Scott is looking at me, I can tell that's not what he meant by "son of Fidel Castro." I can't figure out what he does mean. Does "son of Fidel Castro" mean that Trudeau is a dictator? Does "son of Fidel Castro" mean Trudeau gives speeches that are unnecessarily long? Does "son of Fidel Castro" mean Trudeau has got himself into a fashion rut by refusing to take off an old, unattractive hat?

It turns out that "son of Fidel Castro" means "son of Fidel Castro." Scott opens up his computer. "You know his real father was Fidel Castro. I can't believe you don't know this," he says. I am still confused, since Justin Trudeau wasn't an orphan with unknown parentage. His father was Pierre Trudeau, who was the prime minister of Canada for more than fifteen years.

Or so I thought. Scott shows me photos of Justin Trudeau's mom hanging out with Castro. His next image search brings up pages of side-by-side photos of Justin Trudeau and Fidel Castro that do look similar. Justin Trudeau is the same height as Fidel Castro, but four inches shorter than Pierre Trudeau. It turns out Justin Trudeau's parents' marriage was weird: Pierre and Margaret met when he was forty-eight and she was eighteen, and they eloped while he was prime minister. Margaret Trudeau was bipolar and wrote that she cheated on her husband with Ted Kennedy. Though it turns out that Margaret Trudeau did not meet Fidel Castro until after Justin was born. It also turns out that if two people have enough photos online, you can find pictures in which they both make the same facial expression from the same angle. *SPY* magazine proved this in a feature called "Separated at Birth," which included side-by-side photos of Mick Jagger and Don Knotts. I fear I have started a rumor about Don Knotts and Mick Jagger's mom.

This is addle-brained conspiracy mongering. I tell Scott that this reminds me of when far-right provocateur Milo Yiannopoulos told me that Bill Clinton had a black son.

Scott looks at me like I'm the one who is crazy. "You didn't know about Danney?" he asks. Scott tells me all about Danney Williams, the supposed secret son of Clinton and a prostitute. Danney was only the start of my ignorance about Clinton genealogy. "Chelsea is Webb Hubbell's kid," he says, referring to Bill Clinton's associate attorney general who was imprisoned for fraud. "Look at the pictures." Some of the side-by-side photos of Chelsea Clinton and Webb Hubbell that he shows me were posted on Twitter by Danney Williams.

The myth about Danney was easily disproven in 1999 with Bill Clinton's DNA samples, which are the easiest DNA samples in the world to get. The rumor sprang from the suspicion that elite liberal baby boomers were malleable on issues of sexual morality. But the newer conspiracy theories about Chelsea Clinton and Justin Trudeau's bloodlines didn't stem from panic about prurience, which no one cares about anymore. They were gestated in a new fear about the elite. That we are a tiny, incestuous group that makes secretive deals to enrich each other. Although I find this ridiculous, after doing a lot of photo research I have come to the conclusion that my real father is Charles Schwab and hope he does the honorable thing and acknowledges this in a legally binding way, such as a will or estate plan.

As we look at more pictures of Danney Williams making the same face as Bill Clinton, Scott assures me that he's not a racist. This is something that the people in Miami also told me a lot, which I found weird, because my friends and I are always talking about how racist we are. To prove that his concerns about immigration are nonracist and based on the type of objective facts he has spent all day telling me don't exist, Scott shows me a clip from Tucker Carlson's Fox News show, in which he says that noncitizens commit 22 percent of all murders and 72 percent of all drug possession crimes in the United States. This makes no sense, since only about 7 percent of people living in the United States are noncitizens, and they are apparently way too high to do all that murdering. I take over Scott's keyboard and go on Wikipedia to show him that immigrants commit less crime than citizens. I know it's stupid to litigate statistics with a person who wrote a book subtitled *Persuasion in a World Where Facts Don't Matter*, but I am doing it for me. I will not give up the core of my elite, fact-loving soul.

I thank Scott for being such a good host, and he hands me a tiny refrigerated bottle of water for the road. On my way to the airport, I drive through Pleasanton and get a vanilla soft-serve cone from the smiley teenagers at Meadowlark Dairy. I couldn't understand how Scott, who sees this idyllic version of America every day, wants to tear down the elite who keep it running.

I didn't know that five days earlier, Trump had explained away this paradox in the most unlikely way.

CHAPTER 17

The Boat Elite

At a rally in Duluth, Minnesota, President Trump complimented the elites. This was suprising because it contradicts his campaign rants about defying the "arrogant elite." It also contradicts the strategy of generations of Republicans. In the past eight months, Senate candidates Roy Moore and Todd Rokita both ran on campaigns called Defeat the Elite, standing in front of Defeat the Elite backdrops at speeches, handing out Defeat the Elite signs at rallies, and planting Defeat the Elite placards on lawns. The word *elite* has been so successfully poisoned by Republicans that Reid Hoffman pleaded with me not to use it in this book. When I refused, he suggested qualifying it by coining a term such as "humble elitism" or "open elitism," although I think he would have also approved of "Reid Hoffman is not involved in elitism."

Yet Trump defended the elites to 8,000 cheering fans in a filled arena. "You ever notice they always call the other side 'the elite'? The elite! Why are they elite? I have a much better apartment than they do. I'm smarter than they are. I'm richer than they are. I became president and they didn't," Trump said. "We have more money and more brains and better houses and apartments and nicer boats.... We are the elite!" To most observers, it didn't make sense. It was as if people in Boston started saying, "Technically we're Yankees!"

I, however, was not surprised he was reappropriating the term. It's what Vilfredo Pareto said would happen.

In his 1901 treatise *The Rise and Fall of Elites*, the Italian economist became the first person to use the word *elite* as we do today. He knew the elite well, being the son of a marquis, a talented swordfighter, and the cultivator of a beard so long and full that it must have ruled out any form of manual labor, including feeding himself. His essay put forth the theory of "the circulation of elites," which argues that revolutions don't occur when conditions are so horrible that the masses take to the streets with guitars and papiermâché puppets. They occur whenever one group of elites sees an opportunity to take power from another.

Feudalism, democracy, socialism—these are nothing more than different costumes for the elite. It's George Orwell's *Animal Farm* ("The creatures outside looked from pig to man, and from man to pig, and from pig to man again; but already it was impossible to say which was which") or the Who's anti-hippie anthem "Won't Get Fooled Again" ("Meet the new boss / Same as the old boss"). Pareto expressed the idea even more succinctly: "History is a graveyard of elites." According to his theory, there will always be an elite and, as the Pareto principle states, they'll always make up 20 percent of the population and have 80 percent of the wealth. Admittedly, Pareto's theory of the inexorable power of the elites took a hit a year after his treatise was published when his wife left him for one of his servants.

Pareto posited that the elite circulated between the "speculators," who are innovative, cooperative, sneaky, and everyone I know, and "rentiers," who are tough, loyal, hardworking, tribal, traditional, and are indeed likely to have more money, better houses, and—as Trump pointed out—nicer boats. These people care about boats so much that in 2019 Fox News anchor Sean Hannity railed against a plan to raise taxes by saying, "that means the rich people won't be buying boats that they like recreationally." Like Hannity and Trump, Pareto believed that rentiers should be in charge. I, however, am certain that a society run by people who own boats can't be pleasant. Boat owners are, objectively, bad people. Boat owners are so dangerous that every country has agreed that as soon as they get twelve nautical miles from the shore, they are not our problem, no matter what horrible things they do.

In Minnesota, Trump was announcing the start of the war between the speculators and rentiers. He later called the speculators the "elite" and rentiers like him the "super-elite," because rentiers don't know many words. But since the two sides neatly divide between those who value education over money and those who value money over education, I'm going to call them the Intellectual Elite and the Boat Elite.

The Boat Elite focus on survival: defense, energy, housing, something to keep you from drowning in a large body of water. The Intellectual Elite understand that we've moved farther up Maslow's hierarchy of needs to a stage where experiences and ideas are more important. Populists accuse us of focusing on the frippery of fads in fashion and food. Which are indeed important to us. I ordered a pizza from Papa John's for an article I was writing, and a few minutes later I got an email from Visa's fraud department that had "flagged the purchase as unsusual," by which it meant "disgusting."

We're not obsessed with food, the arts, and fashion. We're just surrounded by it. We live in cities, where, due to density and ambition, all the things the rest of the world will soon enjoy are created. In 1997, when the word *elite* reached its peak use, it was often preceded by the phrase *latte-drinking*. In 2003, Democratic presidential candidate and Vermont governor Howard Dean got destroyed in the Iowa caucus in part due to a negative ad featuring a white, older couple in a town so small the sign for the barber shop said BARBER SHOP. The man in the ad says, "I think Howard Dean should take his tax-hiking, government-expanding, latte-drinking, sushi-eating, Volvo-driving, *New York Times*–reading"—before being interrupted by the woman clutching his arm, who adds, "body-piercing, Hollywood-loving, left-wing freak show back to Vermont, where it belongs." Lattes are now so universal that the anti-immigration hardliner who was Republican chairman of the House Judiciary Committee from 2013 to 2018 did not need to change his name even though it is Bob Goodlatte. The only way to separate populists from their beloved Venti Starbucks cups is to pry them from their cold, dead, shaky hands. For Memorial Day in 2017, the official GOP Twitter feed showcased their "Thanks a latte" project, where they gave frothy beverages to members of Congress who had served in the armed forces. The Boat Elite have infiltrated our high-end coffee society so thoroughly that, in an effort to reestablish our identity, we created a coffee chain called Intelligentsia.

Yes, having a barrista prepare an espresso beverage is more precious than filling a mug from your coffeemaker, but progress always makes us softer. The first time I went to a hipster coffee shop, I noticed that the suspendered, handlebar-mustachioed barista had drawn a heart in the foam of my cortado. This seemed forward of him. Was he going to write his phone number on the back of my receipt? He handed the next guy his cappuccino, which also had a foam heart, as if I suddenly meant nothing to him. Then the woman behind us got her drink and it, too, was foam-hearted. This guy was hitting on anything that drank caffeine. Slowly, I realized that our society had become so civilized that straight men can draw each other hearts just because it's nifty looking. This is an enormous behavioral shift. If you walked through batwing doors into an Old West saloon and a suspendered, handlebar-mustachioed bartender handed you a beer with a heart drawn in the foam, you would hit him over the head with a chair.

The moment in 2008 when I knew I was voting for Barack Obama was when he said, "Anybody gone into Whole Foods lately and seen what they charge for arugula?" Obama was a member of the Intellectual Elite, a worldly Harvard professor with a grasp of the vast complexities of the world, even those that apply to choosing salad greens. One of the tells that Donald Trump isn't an Intellectual Elite is that he eats a lot of fast food. He downs Kentucky Fried Chicken off of china plates on Air Force One and proudly served McDonald's on silver trays next to gold candelabras to the national college football championship team when they visited the White House. Worse, when he's at a restaurant, he orders aged steaks well done and then pours ketchup on them. If he had listened to the expertise offered by chefs, cookbook authors, and food critics instead of relying on his first reaction like a toddler, he would have gotten acclimated to the texture of a medium-rare steak. Then he wouldn't need vinegar sugar to compensate for the moisture and flavor he removed by overcooking it. If Intellectual Elites weren't dedicated to legal principles, they would make well-done steaks the core of their impeachment arguments.

In *Bobos in Paradise*, David Brooks's 2000 book about the Intellectual Elite (whom he Intellectual Elitely calls bourgeois bohemians), he writes, "The following people and institutions fall outside the ranks of Bobo respectability" before listing thirteen Intellectual Elite horrors. The final entry is Hooters, but the first is Donald Trump. And, yes, there are photos of Trump posing with Hooters waitresses. They all stand next to an open briefcase full of cash in an Atlantic City casino at the Donald Trump's Ultimate Deal Cash Giveaway event. Trump topped Brooks's list because he delights in shunning all that the Intellectual Elite hold dear. Trump's big campaign item was a trucker hat. According to Stormy Daniels, he travels with Pert shampoo and Old Spice deodorant. The very accurate title of Anthony Scaramucci's book about his former boss is *Trump, the Blue-Collar President*.

The biggest difference between the two elites is that the Boat Elite are steeped in honor culture. Dignity is their most valuable nonboat possession. If their girl-friend gets insulted, they fight. If their friend gets in a fight, they fight. If their fighting ability is questioned, they fight. When they get cut off, they honk. Then they yell at the other driver to get out of their car and fight. The Intellectual Elite don't do this because we know that honking and yelling makes it hard to hear NPR stories. The Boat Elite are the Real Housewives, throwing their wine at each other's faces at the hint of an insult. The Intellectual Elite would never do that because our wine is too good. More importantly, we wouldn't do it because we value conflict resolution. Besides, we don't mind losing all that much. We fail all the time, without any loss in pride. Silicon Valley's motto is "Fail fast," and tech guys launched FailCon in 2009 so people could brag about how their startups lost millions. We are so into quitting that at Stanford you could drop a class the day before the finals without giving any reason, though the reason was clearly that you were going to get a bad grade. Here's a partial list of things I've quit in my life: the baritone horn, my high-school track team, Mechanical Engineering 101, my political science major, every Dostoyevsky novel I ever started, three jobs, the book I was contracted to write before this one, the rest of this sente

Boat Elite need to win every dispute because they don't understand that cooperation is how our species succeeded. It's a key reason humans and ants have spread out to cover the planet while there are fewer than 5,000 tigers and rhinos left; yet if you were alone on a desert island with a rhinoceros, it would stomp on your precious opposable thumbs. The Boat Elite love to talk about the greatness of "lone wolves," even though wolves die when away from their pack. Biologists David Sloan Wilson and E. O. Wilson wrote, "Selfishness beats altruism within groups. Altruistic groups beat selfish groups." In his book, *Blueprint*, Yale professor Nicholas Christakis argues that our cooperative tendencies, such as our desire to teach each other what we've learned, have helped make us successful, although boring.

The culture wars refer to social issues such as abortion, guns, drug legalization, and gay marriage. But there are also culture wars about the actual culture, and Intellectual Elite are losing them to the Boat Elite despite the fact that we run Hollywood. Stories of cooperation and complexity have been replaced by raw expressions of good and evil, us versus them. Even if Scott is right about us watching two movies on one screen, the odds are that they're both superhero movies. I asked my dad which would have surprised him more about the future when he was a boy in the 1950s: a black president or the fact that most adults would be able to name a dozen comic book characters. He picked the latter. He'd have been shocked to discover that adults read *Harry Potter* and *The Hunger Games* silently, to themselves, without any children around. Sure, the Intellectual Elite won on cappuccinos and teaching kids about Alexander Hamilton, but we have lost on almost everything else.

Scott saw an opportunity to switch elite teams. He took the risk because while he lives in a beautiful town in a beautiful house with a beautiful author of inspirational poems, his problem wasn't different from the one people in Miami, Texas, struggle with. His comic wasn't as huge as it used to be. He was losing power. So he switched elites, from the haves to the have-yachts.

Lots of people are jumping onto the ship. Three days after I leave Scott's house, Justice Anthony Kennedy announces he's retiring and I fear we are about to lose a key member of the Intellectual Elite. Back when he was a circuit judge, Justice Kennedy gave a talk to local judges and lawyers in Alabama in which he explained that he listened to music at home when he read cases. "I have one-opera and two-opera briefs," he said. One of the lawyers in the audience said he wrote briefs in a similar manner. "I have a one-six-pack brief and two-six-pack brief," he said. I fear Trump will replace Justice Kennedy with a two-six-pack-brief judge, someone who appears on Fox News or adjudicated one of his divorces more in his favor than the other judges did. So it's to my great relief when Trump chooses Brett Kavanaugh, who went to Yale undergrad and Yale Law School before clerking for Justice Kennedy and is respected as an Intellectual Elite by both liberal and conservative colleagues.

But right before he is about to be confirmed by the Senate, a research psychologist at Stanford Medical School says Brett Kavanaugh assaulted her when they were in high school. She tells the story of her attack to the Senate Judiciary Committee in a way that brings tears to Intellectual Elite eyes, using phrases such as "multifactorial aetoiologies," the "sequelae of sexual assault," and "indelible in the hippocampus." When Judge Kavanaugh testifies, he jumps elite teams so quickly that only quantum mechanics could explain it. He does what all Boat Elite do when their honor is questioned: he fights. He goes full Boat Elite, roaring with unfiltered instinct. He cries, yells, accuses the Democrats of conspiracy, does not mention opera once, and says that he likes beer more than thirty times. It is challenging to guess which lines below are from Brett Kavanaugh's Senate testimony and which are the lyrics to Alan Jackson's song "Chattahoochee," which had a video featuring the singer wearing cowboy boots and jeans while waterskiing behind a speedboat:

> I spent much of my time
> Working, working out, lifting weights
> Playing basketball, or hanging out
> And having some beers with friends
> As we talked about life and football and school and girls.
>
> —*Brett Kavanaugh, Senate testimony,*
> *September 27, 2018*

Down by the river on a Friday night
A pyramid of cans in the pale moonlight
Talking about cars and dreaming about women
Never had a plan just a living for the minute.

—Alan Jackson, "Chattahooochee,"
May 17, 1993

We will hear arguments next in Beer v. the
United States. Mr. Stoner, you may proceed
whenever you are ready.

—Chief Justice Warren E. Burger,
November 12, 1975

Forty-four years ago, a person named Burger could call on a person named Stoner to talk about a racial redistricting case involving a person named Beer and no one involved would stoop to make a single dumb joke about it.

When Brett Kavanaugh was confirmed, the Boat Elite breached our last line of defense, the Supreme Court. And they are gaining more power. While Scott is the punk pundit of the Boat Elite, firing off bon memes, others on his team are formulating a serious thesis. They are attacking the nerve center of the Intellectual Elite: our devotion to meritocracy.

CHAPTER 18

Tucker

David Bowie and Mick Jagger belt "Dancing in the Street" on the speakers while Tucker Carlson holds my hands as we quick-step around the Third Street Dance studio in Beverly Hills. A couple of weeks later, I go to a party at Tucker's rented house in Los Angeles to watch his debut performance on *Dancing with the Stars*. It consists mostly of him sitting on a chair while his partner dances around him, and I am nervous that when the music ends he will instinctually hand her twenty dollars. But Tucker is looking at the TV and smiling, as if this is going well, even though it clearly isn't. When at the end of the episode he's the first person eliminated from the contest, he isn't at all up-set. He felt like he won simply for being on. Not in a participatory trophy way, but because his appearance made people angry.

Back then, Tucker was an irascible libertarian trickster who was personally well liked by both the left and right. I well liked him, appearing on his show a few times. He was a talented magazine writer and a funny debating partner. But Tucker has since joined the Boat Elite, horrifying his old Intellectual Elite friends. Tucker's rants against immigration, diversity, and the mainstream press led Seth McFarlane, the creator of Fox's *Family Guy*, to say that his ideas are "fringe shit, and it's business like this that makes me embarrassed to work for this company." This was quickly seconded by *Modern Family* creator Steve Levitan and directors Paul Feig and Judd Apatow. If Tucker Carlson ever is in a dark alley in Los Angeles, there's a fair chance that someone will pop out of the shadows and strike him with a hilarious insult.

The drawing on the cover of Tucker's book *Ship of Fools: How a Selfish Ruling Class Is Bringing America to the Brink of Revolution* is a pirate ship, festooned with both Republican red and Democrat blue flags, going over a waterfall. The ship is occupied by eight members of the elite: Hillary Clinton, Republican senators Mitch McConnell and Lindsey Graham, tech CEOs Jeff Bezos and Mark Zuckerberg, Democratic representatives Maxine Waters and Nancy Pelosi, and, leading in the front of the ship, peering through the spyglass, conservative columnist Bill Kristol. He is, of course, the person you put on a book cover if your goal is to sell lots of books to Bill Kristol.

The book's attack on all I value is devastating. The worst is when he refers to *Ulysses*—which I celebrate annually by going to Bloomsday events—as "James Joyce's unreadable modernist novel." It made me want to throw Tucker into the sea, the snotgreen sea, the scrotumtightening sea.

Unlike Scott, Tucker was comfortable being a member of the elite. Tucker Swanson McNear Carlson was raised in La Jolla, a wealthy seaside section of San Diego where the University of California San Diego, the Salk Institute, and the Scripps Institution of Oceanography are located. His father ran the Voice of America, was CEO of the Corporation for Public Broadcasting, and ambassador to the Seychelles. His mom left the family to move to France and become a painter and sculptor, which, as far as elitism is concerned, trumps being an ambassador to the Seychelles. Tucker's stepmother, Senator J. William Fulbright's niece, inherited the Swanson frozen food fortune. Carlson went to boarding school at St. George's School, where Vanderbilts, Astors, and Bushes attended, and where he began his practice of wearing a bow tie every day, which he continued until his midthirties. He summers in Maine, where he makes his own flies for fishing. His first name is Tucker, which is Anglo-Saxon for "white."

"Tucker" actually comes from the Old English word for "torment," because tuckers were workers who beat cloths against water to soften them, which apparently was a job considered complicated enough to name. Tucker decided to torment the Intellectual Elite ten years ago, when he had an epiphany. "It was at a cocktail party in Paris," he says to me, in a sentence Pareto would have loved. "I was talking to a finance guy who was kind of clever but not wise, like most of them. He was an Australian and we were talking about some matter of national sovereignty and he looked at me and said, 'Nationality is just a passport.'" The Australian banker meant that his connection to his country was no greater than the design on the cover of his passport, and if he didn't like the way things were going down under, he'd vote with his Gulfstream jet.

This disturbed Tucker greatly. He figured that only a tiny percentage of American citizens had the money and lack of familial obligations to be able to leave their country. The only people who had this kind of international freedom were the elites. Which meant that the people making the biggest decisions about our nation had no skin in the game. "You need to lash the leadership to the mast of the country or they'll fuck the country," Tucker says. "The problem with globalization is that by definition it works against the nation-state. And that's why everyone who benefits from globalization is for undermining the nation-state. The problem is that everyone else who is stuck in the nation-state gets dicked." Trump won all but one of the twenty-five states with the lowest percentages of passport holders. I'm guessing he won exactly one voter who goes to cocktail parties and starts a conversation about some matter of national sovereignty.

I think back to the night of the presidential election when Cassandra woke me up by reviewing what countries we could escape to. My friend Neil Strauss suggested we buy a second citizenship. If we purchased an apartment costing at least $200,000 on the Caribbean islands of St. Kitts and Nevis, we could get a passport through that country's "citizenship by investment" policy. He took out this insurance policy years ago and had no regrets. Except for the morning he woke up in the St. Kitts apartment he bought for his own safety and saw a thief breaking in through the window. When I turned down this plan, Neil suggested that he and I instead become "perpetual travelers," which we could do thanks to our lack of office jobs, moving from country to country every six months. "We wouldn't be going and hiding but growing and experiencing," he said. "We'll bring our nanny." Neil and I were indeed not lashed to America's mast. If Tucker had read *Ulysses*, his least favorite part might have been when elitist Stephen Dedalus, who teaches ancient Greek history, turns drunkenly toward a soldier and says, "Let my country die for me."

The leadership we must lash to the mast, Tucker argues, should indeed consist of experts. This is the part of the new Boat Elite philosophy that Scott had not been briefed on. "The federal government is the most complex human organization ever created. I've lived in DC since I was fifteen, my dad worked for the government, and I don't know how it works," he says. It's not a fog that no one understands, but thousands of fiefdoms staffed by the few people who have the requisite knowledge. Tucker also believes that the leaders of these fiefdoms are bright. The top colleges have done a decent job of filtering and connecting a tiny group of people with intellectual rigor. I find his position on this to be a great relief. No two movies. No pretending the Fed does nothing.

Then Tucker tells me about the Intellectual Elite's faults. One is that we aren't as smart as we think we are. That led us to believe we could fix Iraq and hedge risks on loans efficiently enough that banks could give mortgages to people for houses they could never afford. This was standard Meteorologist Fallacy™ stuff.

But Tucker argues that our intellectual hubris pales in comparison to our bigger problem. We are real jerks. This is the core of the attack against meritocracy. The Intellectual Elite believe we earned our status by scoring well on a standardized test when we were seventeen. I, for instance, still remember that I got a 1480 on my SATs. That entitlement stripped us of the noblesse oblige felt by the previous elites, who were born into their positions. Those aristocrats knew they lucked into power and could never have scored a 1480 on their SATs, which is the score I got. So they felt like they owed a debt for their luck, which they paid back to the masses through museums, universities, libraries, orchestras, and other things that the masses don't enjoy. Meanwhile, the meritocratic elite don't feel like we owe anything. The word *meritocracy* that we elitists proudly wield as a shield against attacks on our legitimacy was coined as a pejorative by Michael Young, a sociologist who became the secretary of the policy committee of the Labour Party and a member of the House of Lords. His 1958 dystopian novel, *The Rise of the Meritocracy*, ends in 2034, when dissident Boat Elite lead the people who suck at college entrance exams in a revolt against the smug London Intellectual Elite bastards who believe they deserve their status because they're good at penciling in bubbles.

The Intellectual Elite's false belief that we earned our status robbed us of empathy and wisdom. Tucker argues that these are the traits most important to leadership. Eric Garcetti might think Trump is a disaster for driving a truck without the brains to do it, but Tucker thinks Hillary was unfit to lead because she didn't have a heart. We didn't so much have an election as the second act of *The Wizard of Oz*.

The idea that former elites were filled with noblesse oblige, however, isn't historically accurate. Noblesse oblige is the theory animating the White Man's Burden, which justified colonization. We didn't feel a lot of noblesse oblige from King George III when he raised taxes on stamps and tea, which threw us into a fury even though those are the two things Americans care least about. And plenty of the Intellectual Elite nobles are obliging. The Giving Pledge where Reid Hoffman promised to donate more than half his money has 190 signatories, nearly all billionaire members of the Intellectual Elite. Donald Trump is not on the list. Neither is Lynn D. Stewart, the founder of Hooters.

It isn't new to claim the educated are unfit for leadership because we lack emotions. Baynard Rush Hall was a minister trained at Princeton Theological Seminary who moved to Indiana to be the first professor at what is now Indiana University, where he taught Greek and Latin. In his 1843 book about his life as a member of the East Coast elite living on the frontier, *The New Purchase: Or, Seven and a Half Years in the Far West*, he wrote:

> We always preferred an ignorant bad man to a talented one…and hence attempts were usually made to ruin the moral character of a smart candidate; since unhappily smartness and wickedness were supposed to be generally coupled, and incompetence and goodness.

More than one hundred years later, in 1962, Richard Hofstadter made the same observation in *Anti-Intellectualism in American Life*:

Intellect is pitted against feeling, on the ground that it is somehow inconsistent with warm emotion. It is pitted against character, because it is widely believed that intellect stands for mere cleverness, which transmutes easily into the sly or diabolical.

One reason this attack on the Intellectual Elite is used a lot is that it's a little true. Psychological studies consistently show that people who went to college show less empathy than mere high-school graduates. Knowing we can hire strangers to watch our kids or drive us to the hospital prevents us from building the connections poorer communities have, causing an empathy deficit. It's a problem summed up by Judge Rick Tennant when he asked whether I'd trust everyone within half a mile of my house to watch my son.

The Intellectual Elite's great failure of empathy, the one that animates Tucker's fury, was our failure to react to the moment in 2015 when our country stopped being predominantly middle class. Globalization may have led to an economic boom saving billions of lives—the percent of the world population living in extreme poverty is 75 percent lower than it was 1990; about 80 percent as many children under five die as in 1960—but it has shoved a wedge into developed countries. It has hurt the middle class, who toil in the industrial and service economies and compete with workers all over the world while enriching the elite, who work in the knowledge economy and manipulate the global flow of activity. I could be giving money to help these people in my nation-state, but my extraordinarily limited philanthropy has not been America First. Most of it has gone to Kiva, where I recirculate microloans to female entrepreneurs in developing nations. I recently lent $225 to Neelavathi, an Indian mom and day laborer, so she can buy more straw for her side gig making straw mats. I feel smart about my choice. This is a woman whose dilemma is not having straw. That's something I can fix. Plus, I admire her hardworking, entrepreneurial spirit. She makes things out of straw. You know what I do when I happen upon free straw? I walk around it, because who knows what's lying underneath straw? I've never seen straw and thought, *I should start a business!*

I might be a dick for lacking empathy for American opioid addicts, but Tucker is an even bigger dick for shunning refugees from Syria's civil war. The biblical quote on the wall of the room where Jerry ran our Bible study said, "Be not forgetful to entertain strangers. For some have entertained angels unaware." It didn't say to forget strangers if they're from another country. Putting America first is selfish considering that we're already first in GDP, currency reserves, military spending, medical research, movies, tech, natural gas production, and international calling code numbers. Nationalism is cruel. In his 1945 essay "Notes on Nationalism," George Orwell defined nationalism as "the habit of identifying oneself with a single nation or other unit, placing it beyond good and evil and recognizing no other duty than that of advancing its interests."

Globalization is only negative when you look at it myopically with your gut instead of with data that shows how much wealth it's brought to the world. But Tucker says that the elite have a special responsibility to the country that gave them their success. It's irresponsible to buy straw for foreigners while refusing to even hire American-born Americans as my gardeners and house-cleaners. "The elites said, 'Fine, we'll just import Hondurans.' It's easier to import a serf class. They're not making all kinds of demands. They just do what they're told and go to some trailer park at night," he says. Petra Köpping, the liberal minister in charge of integrating immigrants in the economically troubled blue collar German state of Saxony, made the same point in her book *First, Integrate Us!*, whose title came from what a furious middle-aged white man screamed at her.

I'm talking to Tucker by phone from my liberal mom's house on the New Jersey shore, where a team of skinny white American-born Americans who have a Trump sticker on their pickup truck are rebuilding her deck. They don't usually show up. When they do, my mom's husband, a former social worker, tries to help them with their issues, which have included drug addiction, prison time, parents who abandoned them, and lawsuits over who owns the family business. My mom, also a former social worker, avoids them because she's infuriated by their Trump sticker. After going over budget, the workers do not think they will be able to finish the deck after three months of trying. My deck, meanwhile, was built in days by my friendly, talented gardeners who are from Mexico and never tell me about their problems. The two Latin American immigrant women who clean our house every other week don't speak enough English for me to know what their problems are or apparently, exactly, which country they're from. I have been to gatherings on my block about how to defeat Trumpism and fight for diversity, but every single person who lives on this block is either white or Asian. The only Latino or black people I see on my street are here to garden, clean houses, do construction, or push white babies in strollers. Maybe Pareto was right. Maybe I deserve to be circulated. Though I can't help but think that people who say they can build a deck should be able to build a deck.

Hiring foreigners we don't have much in common with, Tucker says, has distanced the Intellectual Elite from the rest of the nation. I don't even see the middle class anymore. A generation ago, the upper class lived in the same towns, ate in the same restaurants, went to the same churches, and belonged to the same organizations as the middle class. Even though both Tucker and I grew up with money, we stayed at Holiday Inns on vacations and ate at McDonald's so regularly that I actually won things in that peel-off Monopoly game. My son has never been to a McDonald's. When Cassandra bought an Egg McMuffin at an airport last year, he cried and begged her not to eat it, fearful of the consequences.

We elite have walled ourselves off from the rest of the country. After finding a pair of women's underwear and a used condom on our lawn, Cassandra sat me down to discuss having an actual wall built outside our home, which seemed a deeply hypocritical move for a woman horrified by Trump's call to build a wall on the Mexican border. I objected, but avoided a long argument for fear that she'd start to wonder if I had anything to do with the underwear and condom. Ever since then, Cassandra points to each house in our neighborhood and declares, "That's a secure home!" or "That's not a secure home!" So I knew I was in trouble when our homeowners' association asked us to contribute seventy-five dollars a month toward a private neighborhood patrol service called ACS. If enough of us joined, armed security guards would drive around our streets twenty-four hours a day in vehicles with sirens and apprehend anyone they suspected of criminal behavior. I have no idea why hiring a paramilitary organization is legal, since, as we've established in this book's introduction, the Constitution states that only Congress can grant letters of marque and reprisal. Even if it is legal, it's weird that our neighborhood's disgust with guns does not extend to having other people wield them for us. When Jerry asked me during Bible study what I did when I saw homeless people, I didn't think my answer would be "Call in guys with fake badges to scare them away." I can get really worked up about spending seventy-five dollars a month.

Still, I should not have been surprised when I walked into our house and saw Cassandra signing a contract with a guy in a fake cop suit. I am surprised, however, a few weeks later when Cassandra wakes me at 2:00 a.m. She says there are people with flashlights on the deck right outside our bedroom door. I see the beams of light swirling around and assure her that they're coming from helicopters above. She does not buy this explanation, since it's clearly not true. Also, helicopter searchlights circling our deck would be equally scary. I head nervously to the glass doors and the flashlights dart away. So, like a real man who wants to get his seventy-five dollars' worth, I call ACS.

When someone knocks on the door, I check outside the windows and see three police officers laughing. When I open the door, however, they do not look happy. They inform us that our next-door neighbors asked their security company—a different one called Post—to inspect their yard while they were out of town, which they were doing vigilantly with flashlights. After the annoyed cops left, the ACS guards showed up and inspected our backyard to make extra sure everything was copacetic. When they went into our backyard with their flashlights, I feared the neighbors on the other side of our house were going to call their security service—Bel Air—and all three security services would start shooting each other in an internecine war. After the entire neighborhood's corpses were carted away, Bernie Sanders would redistribute our houses to the middle class.

Tucker believes the only way to fix this anomie is to reduce income inequality. This is not what conservatives are supposed to say. They're supposed to talk about trickling down and the Laffer curve, which is a graph that claims it's okay for rich people to laugh at poor people. "Socialism and communism keep reoccurring as ideas even though they don't work. Why is that? Because the impulse underneath them is right. The egalitarian society is the goal, always," Tucker says, in opposition to everything his party once believed in.

I respect Tucker's impulse for localized wealth equality, but tossing out our entire leadership seems like an overreaction to a roaring, low-unemployment US economy that's the opposite of the Great Depression. "It's so much worse than the Depression," Tucker says. "Poverty doesn't cause social unrest. You look at any agrarian society where people are eating weeds and dirt and they're actually very stable societies." This may be because dirt eaters don't have a lot of energy to revolt. Though I'm sure I could get poor people to revolt if I told them Tucker Carlson said, "Let them eat weeds and dirt!" But I do have to admit that Miami, Texas, coalesced as a community partly because, unlike in Los Angeles, all the houses were similar in size.

But the hypothesis that jealousy causes revolution doesn't make sense, because many angry populists are Christian evangelicals and the Tenth Commandment is "Thou shall not covet." Also, black middle-class factory workers weren't economically anxious enough to vote for Trump or Brexit. People aren't angry at the Intellectual Elite for our money, but for our lifestyles. While the large political parties put economic issues at the top of their campaign platforms from 1950 to 1983, when US income disparity was smaller, social issues have dominated since then. I'm also dubious because conservatives are voting to lower their taxes, the main way to redistribute wealth.

The populist philosopher king, however, is willing to jettison the Intellectual Elite conservatives and their disdain for redistribution. "Do I have some moral obligation to stick up for every corporate douchebag in the world? I kind of feel like I do because I grew up a right-winger and you have to defend business. But why? They don't care about me or my family, or share my values. Fuck them!" Tucker says before laughing. It's the laugh of freedom. The laugh of abandoning your old tribe for one in ascendance. The laugh of a man on the high seas with wind in his hair and a flag that reads VIVA LA CIRCULACIÓN!

The Boat Elite, however, don't want to improve wealth inequality by raising taxes. That's the kind of fix Intellectual Elites come up with because they care more about influence than money. The Boat Elite advocate fixing local wealth inequality by overthrowing the entire rigged, faux-meritocratic system, which is beyond repair. The political riots that are upon us are the fault of the Intellectual Elite, who ran the boat over the cliff on the cover of Tucker's book. "A healthy country would not even consider electing Donald Trump. There are a lot of people in this country. Why would you pick him? It's a terrible sign. It's not an attack on him. If America elected me president it would be a terrible sign. If you're electing TV show hosts, something is wrong. The check-engine light has gone on. You ought to pull over immediately," Tucker says.

But the elite didn't pull over and open the hood, he says. There was no moment of introspection. No task force to solve the problem of the declining life expectancy of the middle class. No massive campaign to end opioid addiction, which, a few months after I interviewed Scott Adams, killed his eighteen-year-old stepson. "A wise person will ask, 'If my wife ran off with the mailman, why did she do that?' Maybe I wasn't the husband I thought I was. Maybe I should change. Donald Trump is America running off with the mailman. Nobody at whom that message was aimed received it. They hate Americans for voting for Trump. It's the ugliest thing I've ever seen in my life. The gut reaction of the beneficiaries of the globalized economy was to blame the people whose suffering gave rise to Trump." I think Tucker is being a little hard on guys whose wives sleep with mail carriers; their wives, I'm guessing, are simply intoxicated by the uniform, life on the open road, and the opportunity to drive with the steering wheel on the wrong side without having to travel to England.

What galls Tucker most, judging by the rising volume of his voice, is that the elitists simplified the issue by calling populists racist. This may be because Tucker has been accused of making racist jokes due to the fact that when he was a regular guest for five years on a Tampa, Florida, radio show hosted by Bubba the Love Sponge, he made racist jokes. Whatever his reasons, Tucker makes a good argument that angrily dismissing all populist complaints as mere racism is lazy. It's understandable for the uneducated Trump voter to rage, but the Intellectual Elite should use our algorithms instead of our middle fingers. It's another example of our lack of noblesse oblige. "One of my smartest kids is like that. I say to her, 'I understand you don't like Trump, but you've got this million-dollar education and a really high IQ, so maybe you should be more thoughtful. People are mad for a reason.' She says, 'They're racist.' I say, 'Oh, God. I can't believe I spent good money to send you to college.'"

At another Resistance Party at Stephanie Miller's house, the musician Jill Sobule sat in the living room, leading Lawrence O'Donnell, Moby, Lily Tomlin, songwriter Diane Warren, and a dozen other liberals as we sang her protest anthem, "America Back," which pins Trump's rise on homophobia and racism.

> *When they say*
> *"We want our America Back*
> *Our America back*
> *Our America back*
> *Our America back"*
> *What the fuck do they mean?*
> *Before the gays had their agenda*
> *Before the slaves were free*
> *Before that man from Kenya*
> *Took the presidency*

It wasn't a conspiracy theory, but it had all the benefits of one: there were bad guys, good guys, and a simple solution to a complicated problem. Which was to get rid of racism. So not that simple. Still, the blaming felt good.

The elite don't want to hear Tucker say that it's lazy to dismiss Trump voters as racist. But they might listen to the same argument from Joan C. Williams, the feminist Berkeley law professor who created Gender Bias Bingo, which is the only form of bingo even less fun than regular bingo. Like Tucker, Joan C. Williams warns against "using racism as a mute button" to ignore the loss of social honor at the core of the populist revolution. In the *Harvard Business Review*, which is the most Intellectually Elite–titled publication in the world, she wrote: "To write off white working class anger as nothing more than racism is intellectual comfort food." It's not only her. Despite what Tucker says, a fair number of the people in the Loop have noticed the check-engine light is on. Reid Hoffman said to me, "One of the things I learned from the 2016 election was a lot of it was a 'Hey, fucking pay attention to us.' I find it painful but I respect it. That's a good reminder to me that, oh right, what's super important to you about economic policy is a believable path forward to be successful for you and your children, and that I should make sure I'm factoring that into what I'm doing."

But being right about the cause of their unhappiness does not mean the populists are also correct about the solutions. Especially the ones that Scott Adams proposed. "The part that scares me is alternative facts, science doesn't matter, there is no such thing as truth, it's all conspiracy, going to hate instead of love. If I believe the primacy of my belief over truth, that's a disaster. Truth is a working theory. It's a pretty good theory," Reid says.

Tucker thinks the middle class will never accept any ideas for improving their situation that come from Reid or anyone at an elite conference, no matter how useful they are. Because they can tell we don't respect them. They feel it when we berate them for not knowing to say "transgendered person" instead of "tranny" in a display of cultural superiority they find indistinguishable from telling them they shouldn't drink chardonnay that's heavily oaked. When you don't believe someone respects you, it's hard to trust their motives when they tell you to change. "You can be the greatest pulmonary surgeon in the world, but if I don't trust that you are, I'm not going to let you operate on me. Once you lose trust you're not going to get it back," he says.

The populist philosopher king was going to end his book with a prescription for how to fix our democracy, but he decided there isn't one. "There weren't any democracies between the fall of Rome and the United States," Tucker says. "That's nearly two thousand years. Why is that? It's possible that in a country moving toward four hundred million people pretty fast, it's hard to come to wise decisions in a democracy. You don't practice democracy for its own sake; you practice it because you think it works best. It's possible it doesn't really work at this scale."

I can't believe he said this. It's my greatest fear about the goal of antielitism. Banishing democracy from America's capital is insane because the architecture would make no sense. Kids would be touring Washington, DC, saying, "Daddy, why do all the buildings look like they're in ancient Greece?" And dads would respond, "Yo bro, no one knows. Must have been a fad, like the way new buildings now look like Ultimate Fighting Championship octagons." It's also insane because countries without democracies are hellholes. Dictators are as sadistic as gym teachers, which is why they're always making everybody march. If democracies played nondemocracies in a football game, nondemocracies would get trounced because many of their players would be killed by their own coach. But there's a more fundamental reason Tucker's question about democracy is flawed. You do practice democracy for its own sake. It's not a tool you choose because it delivers more money, more happiness, or even more peace. You choose democracy because freedom, human rights, and self-government are moral goods. If those goods have a price, we should be happy to pay it.

America has no meaning without democracy. *Un-French* might mean "gluten-free," and *un-German* might mean "smiling," but *un-American* means "undemocratic." If you want to expunge democracy from the center of America's identity, you must want to replace it with something else. I worry about what that something is. I figure Tucker soured on democracy because he was the first contestant viewers voted out on *Dancing with the Stars*. But democracy bashing is a key tenet of populism. Democracy isn't cool anymore. Only 40 percent of humanity lives in free societies—a number that has gone down every year since 2006, according to Freedom House, which titled its 2017 report *Democracy in Crisis*. Back in 1995, a little less than 12 percent of Americans said that having a democratic system is "bad" or "very bad"; by 2011 that number had nearly doubled. While 72 percent of Americans born before World War II give a 10 out of 10 for living in a democracy, only about 30 percent of people born after 1980 do; the same numbers were found in Britain, Australia, and New Zealand. This is new. Twenty years ago, young adults liked democracy more than older people who, as a rule, don't like anything. And nearly 40 percent of Americans who didn't graduate college say that they want a "strong leader unchecked by elections and Congress." The share of Americans who think it would be "good" or "very good" to have the army run the country went from 1 in 16 in 1995 to 1 in 6 in 2014.

What populists don't like isn't democracy but republics, which are built to tamp down the majority's will by protecting minorities and human rights. Majorities don't like this, since they were sold a political system where they get whatever they want, right away, damn everyone else. So they tend to turn to tyranny, which is a more efficient form of government. Plato predicted this in *The Republic*. It's the job of the elitist to explain this to people without mentioning Plato's *Republic*.

I'll try this: believing you're so right that you deserve everything you want leads you to resent the groups whose rights get in your way. This leads you to idolize an authoritarian from your tribe who will grab what you believe is rightfully yours. I before we except after he.

The elite, with our pesky qualifiers and annoying exceptions, are the thin line between democracy and tyranny. After fleeing Nazi Germany, the novelist Thomas Mann traveled across America in 1938, rallying people with a speech called "The Coming Victory of Democracy," in which he talked about how attacking the elite leads to tyranny:

> There exists a caricature of this modern anti-intellectualism which has nothing whatever to do with democracy, but which lands us in the middle of the base demagogic world of fascism. This is the contempt of pure reason, the denial and violation of truth in favor of power and the interests of the state, the appeal to the lower instincts, to so-called "feeling," the release of stupidity and evil from the discipline of reason and intelligence, the emancipation of blackguardism. In short, a barbaric mob-movement, beside which what we call democracy certainly stands out as aristocratic to the highest degree.

Jacob Burckhardt, the nineteenth-century Swiss art historian who is so elite he's on the face of the country's largest-denomination bill, which is worth $1,000, called dictators "terrible simplifiers" and said that "the essence of tyranny is the denial of complexity." Democracy is a government of the nerds, by the nerds, and for the nerds. And the Boat Elite do not respect nerds. When I asked germaphobic Donald Trump why he proffered his hand to shake after I interviewed him, he looked me over and said, "What am I going to catch from you?" I look like a guy who no one would bother giving a downtown souvenir.

As the democracy-detesting Boat Elite take power with their fun memes and claim that instincts are more valuable than expertise acquired through our beloved rule of 10,000 hours of hard work, I wonder if anyone still wants to be a member of the Intellectual Elite. If it's possible to reinspire people about the benefits of meritocracy. I wonder if there's some noblesse I need to oblige. I am sure there is. Though I might need to go to a time-traveling store to get there.

PART IV

The Elite Populists

Prudence, indeed, will dictate that Governments long established should not be changed for light and transient causes; and accordingly all experience hath shewn, that mankind are more disposed to suffer, while evils are sufferable, than to right themselves by abolishing the forms to which they are accustomed.

— Thomas Jefferson, United States
Declaration of Independence, 1776

CHAPTER 19

The Time Travel Mart

Harold Stone had kindness in his heart when he gave me the cross he carved out of a book. But a massacred book is a harsh gift to give an author. Though I will happily sell copies of *In Defense of Elitism* to whittlers.

It wasn't any book he destroyed, either. It was a Reader's Digest Condensed Book, a relic of the Intellectual Elite's lost empire. Launched in 1950, these were bibles for Intellectual Elite missionaries, who took them from New York City to convert the vast suburbs. Every two months, 1.5 million subscribers received a volume containing three books by serious authors—William Faulkner, Pearl S. Buck, John Steinbeck, Shirley Jackson, Herman Wouk—that were destroyed by shortening them by up to 50 percent and removing all cursing, sex, violence, and politics. Again, though, feel free to buy this book and do that to it. Reader's Digest didn't only evangelize for great literature. They also created a subscription for albums of classical music with nonthreatening titles without "opus number"s or "in B minor"s or "bagatelles." Titles such as *The Romantic Rachmaninoff* and *Great Music's Greatest Hits*.

Suburbanites thrilled at being included in the Intellectual Elite conversation, even if they were confused about why the members of Faulkner's Compson family were so mopey, considering nothing awful happened to them like forced castration or incestuous lust. They were eager to enter the aristocracy that had been flattened by capitalism. The participants in this neo-Enlightenment were called the middlebrow, but they identified more with highbrow culture than lowbrow entertainment. They joined the Book of the Month Club, which sent out works by authors who sometimes went on to win Nobels or Pulitzers; the key selling point was that the books were selected by six intellectuals who met over glasses of brandy in a wood-paneled office. By watching Dick Cavett and reading *Time* magazine, a huge swath of America was having the same conversations as the elites. In 1949, *Life* magazine ran a two-page chart listing the affectations of the middlebrows. The "lower middle brow" read book club selections, played bridge, and listened to light opera.

Two years after Reader's Digest printed its first condensed book, Eisenhower beat Stevenson, the epithet *egghead* was coined, and the attack on the Intellectual Elite began. The middlebrow slowly withered. Everything the Intellectual Elite is into became labeled as self-important indulgence: majoring in the humanities, reading novels, watching foreign films, listening to classical music, reading anything that's not a text message. Yes, the elite have stopped eating at McDonald's and staying at Holiday Inns, but the middle class has stopped watching movies in which none of the characters have the power of flight.

Even the people who are in the middlebrow now refuse the term. They don't want to be sullied by any connection to the elites. Cassandra's dad, Ken Barry, is totally middlebrow: he watches a lot of PBS, listens to NPR, convinced me to read *Guns, Germs, and Steel*, goes to a museum in every place he visits, and uses his spare time to paint in a studio. The guy owns a tiny winery in upstate New York with his son. Ken hates Trump more than former Trump cabinet members. But Ken does not want to be associated with the elite. Because, like Scott Adams, he thinks they're con artists. He thinks that meritocracy is a scam.

To Ken, an elite conference is another version of a country club designed to keep outsiders out of power. Only instead of being accepted based on your last name, you are accepted based on the name of the college you went to. And colleges are the biggest country clubs. The most popular of the fifteen seasons of Donald Trump's *The Apprentice* was the one that pitted college graduates ("book smarts") against those who didn't finish college ("street smarts"). An overwhelming 72 percent of viewers were rooting for street smarts, though I believe that number is skewed by the fact that no one with book smarts would watch *The Apprentice*. The audience was disappointed, however, because Team Book Smarts won. But they were satisfied that, as they expected, they didn't win because they were smarter. They won because they knew the ways of the modern country club. The college grads won the contest to sell rooms in a Jersey Shore motel they renovated not through accounting or marketing. They did it by throwing a killer opening party. Danny Kastner of the winning team explained that they were able to do it because they spent so much time in college blowing off classes to party.

There's no meritocracy, Ken argues, when college buddies give each other all the sweet jobs. "Tell me there's not a lot of talented people who can head these corporations?" he asks. But there aren't enough talented people with experience who can. The fact that the average lifespan of a company on the S&P 500 is fewer than twenty years proves that there aren't as many people who can take over multinational corporations as there are multinational corporations. Bob Iger has had to postpone his retirement as CEO of Disney twice because the board can't find a successor despite the fact that their customers are prepubescent. Any movie is good enough for them. Then they'll buy toys based on that movie. You know how good a movie for adults has to be to sell merchandise based on it? I have yet to be in someone's bedroom and see a pillow shaped like the dead-horse head from *The Godfather*.

What's strange about this loss of faith in meritocracy is that the meritocracy is more meritocratic than ever. Not long ago the pond meritocracy fished in was very small and very white. Students at Ivy League schools have never been more diverse as measured by gender, race, sexuality, parental income, country of origin, and every other gauge besides political party affiliation. I wouldn't get into Stanford if I applied today. Not only because it would be creepy to have a forty-seven-year-old dude in your frosh dorm, but also because the vast array of people I'd be competing against would make my excellent work as vice president of my Model United Nations club seem less impressive. Elitism was so un-meritocratic in the 1960s that the University of Pennsylvania accepted Donald Trump.

Unfortunately, our meritocracy is still horrifyingly imperfect. Raj Chetty, an economist at Harvard, found that kids with parents whose income is in the top 1 percent are 77 times more likely to go to an Ivy League school than those with parents in the bottom 20 percent. We are tossing away what Chetty calls "lost Einsteins." Still, it's not as if those stats were ferreted out by a professor at Florida A&M University. The meritocracy is even more unfair on a global level. If you have the kind of genius brain that could cure cancer but you're born in rural sub-Saharan Africa, there's a good chance you'll die from cancer. If you're a female genius in Saudi Arabia who could cure cancer, there's a good chance you'll die from your husband beating you.

Back when the unfairness was worse, it didn't turn people off as much. Free public education was uncommon in 1866, when Horatio Alger, a middle-class kid who went to Harvard, wrote children's books celebrating the American Dream. He told the story of Ragged Dick Hunter, a homeless orphan shoeshine boy who seeks an education from Henry Fosdick. Other Alger characters include Tattered Tom, Phil the Fiddler, Chester Rand, Victor Vain, Randy of the River, and Joe the Hotel Boy. Apparently, Alger had gotten hold of a prototype of a gay-porn-star-name generator. These homoerotically named characters weren't part of rags-to-riches tales. They were part of rags-to-middle-class tales. Ragged Dick quits smoking, gambling, and drinking and becomes an accountant to clients who undoubtedly get audited when the government sees their taxes were filed by "Ragged Dick."

The Horatio Alger of our time, which I mean in the nicest way, is Joel Arquillos. He sells meritocracy to the Ragged Dicks of LA by running the Los Angeles branches of 826, the charity started by author Dave Eggers to tutor underprivileged kids in writing. Joel is a genius at making the Loop seem attainable. One of the songs that students wrote in the songwriting workshop was used in a Judd Apatow film. Each year, he publishes a collection of the students' best writing. The books have been quoted in the *New York Times* and are sold at the stores attached to his tutoring centers, where they are sometimes bought by 826LA advisory board members such as J. J. Abrams, Judd Apatow, Miranda July, and Fiona Apple. "Publishing books written by these young people brings them into the conversation," Joel says. "The conversation" is a phrase the Intellectual Elite use to refer to whatever the Intellectual Elite are talking about, which is usually based on an article in the *New Yorker* but sometimes an article in the *New York Times* and occasionally an article in *New York* magazine.

Joel also makes the Intellectual Elite look fun. You have to walk through a store to enter the front of the Sunset Boulevard tutoring center. That store is the Time Travel Mart, which sells food pills for homesick time travelers coming from the future, and Viking Odorant for travelers from the past. There's also a huge display of the cosmos on one wall, though the only connection between time travel and space exploration I can figure out is marijuana.

Joel is thin, tall, smiley, bespectacled, prone to wearing hipster hats, and two weeks younger than I am. That's not all we have in common. We are both from New Jersey, both have one kid, both have the same first name, and are both extraordinarily handsome. We run in somewhat similar elite circles, with forty-six mutual friends according to Facebook, including author Susan Orlean and NPR contributor Starlee Kine.

However, Joel grew up farther from the Loop than I did. His parents are religious, Trump-supporting Baptist immigrants who still pray for him to go to church. His high-school religious teachers warned him to be careful in college because professors taught dangerous lies that could damn his soul. His mom pushed him to go to college nearby at Montclair State University in New Jersey, fearing he would falter without his extended family nearby. But something drove him to seek out the Intellectual Elite. He has been bottling that something and selling it at 826LA, sometimes at the Time Travel Mart in a jar marked "Five More Minutes on Your Expired Parking Meter."

Joel ignored his mom and went to Pace University in Manhattan. "I felt like I wanted to be near the city. That something bigger was happening there," he said. "I was definitely drawn to improving my social status." He couldn't afford to keep living in his Pace dorm, so after a semester he dropped out and moved home, depressed to be pushed away from the Loop. But, even though he was underage, Joel landed a job bartending in Manhattan and found some roommates to live with in Hoboken, New Jersey, while he went to Hunter College in Manhattan. Still, he couldn't quite get into the Loop. "I felt like I missed out on a four-year-college experience. That's where a lot of elitism is born. I only have one to two people from college I stay in touch with. And they're not entrepreneurs," he says.

Still searching for a way into the Loop, Joel moved to San Francisco, where he started a punk band, married a photographer from Japan, and got a job teaching high school social studies at a school full of underprivileged kids. He ran a program called Advancement Via Individual Determination, which is what Horatio Alger would have titled his book if he sucked at writing. This is where Joel learned how to sell meritocracy.

It's not that Joel thinks our meritocracy is giving the kids he works with a fair shot. It didn't give him a fair shot. But he doesn't want to tear it down like the populists do. He believes he can improve it from within, by injecting the elite with kids from less-privileged backgrounds who understand our meritocracy's flaws. And I want to help him.

Theodore Roosevelt High School is 98.7 percent Latino; 97.2 percent of the students are economically disadvantaged. Only 5 percent of the kids who grow up in this neighborhood graduate from four-year colleges. There's a Planned Parenthood–run clinic right inside the school that gives out condoms, though this is not why the sports teams are named the Rough Riders. It's because the school is named after Theodore Roosevelt, a Manhattan-born, son-of-a-socialite-and-a-philanthropist, Harvard-attending, history-book-writing, monocle-wearing elitist who fought to make government hiring and starting a business more meritocratic.

At the school's College and Career Center, I'm paired with William Jimenez, a thin, quiet, sweet kid who I like for many reasons, only one of which is the fact that he gave me permission to write about him. I'm going to help him write his essays for college. He is lucky to have gotten me, assuming he wants to go to the University of Mediocre Jokes Tacked onto the Ends of Paragraphs.

I struggle with William for a while, because he's trying to write what he assumes the Intellectual Elite want to hear. His parables of sports (Teamwork! Determination!) and academics (Rugged Individualism! Determination!) are generic. So I ask William why he wants to go to college. Does he believe the system is meritocratic enough to let him into the elite? What type of elite does he want to join?

Asking questions for your book is not technically helping someone. So I come back the following week and focus on William, bringing him a burrito because he never bothers having lunch. While we're eating, I notice that the lanyard holding the keys that hang around his neck is from Bad Boys Bail Bonds, a service whose motto is "Because your momma wants you home!"™ William's family is going to bail out his brother later today. His home life is crowded and volatile. He quit soccer because he didn't have a ride home and it's too dangerous to walk through his gang-controlled neighborhood. His best friend, who lived three doors down from him, was shot and killed. The point is, William has it way easier as far as college-essay fodder is concerned than I had it. I had to go with that weak "my parents smoked marijuana" thing.

While William's neighborhood is dominated by drug dealers striving to become Boat Elite, William wasn't interested in that path. The ones who climbed up the gang ladder had the same lives they did before, only with more stuff. William didn't want stuff. He wanted a bigger life, which was anything outside of this neighborhood. College is a way to get out, like it was for Joel and me. And I know William will get out, partly because of his determination but mostly because I made that essay sing.

Selling meritocracy is not impossible. It requires the Intellectual Elite to leave our paramilitary-protected neighborhoods and make the case that we're not jerks trying to keep others out. Which is a complicated argument to make when you hire a paramilitary to keep others out of your neighborhood.

William gave me great hope in the future of the Intellectual Elite. I can see him coming home from work to his suburban house and rocking out to *Great*

Music's Greatest Hits while reading a fifty-page version of *Ulysses*. I see all this clearly, thanks to items I purchased at the Time Travel Mart. But I also see a different future. One where after William gets to college, he turns against the Intellectual Elite. Because while we can still recruit people, we're losing a lot of them right after they join.

The far left is becoming populist. They subscribe to the tribalism of identity politics. They question the knowability of truth. And, based on the little I know about Greenpeace, they love boats.

Like Scott Adams, liberal senator Bernie Sanders doesn't think much of mainstream economics. He argued in an essay that the Federal Reserve Board should include "representatives from all walks of life—including labor, consumers, homeowners, urban residents, farmers and small businesses." Imagine if farmers were on the Federal Reserve Board, spending all their time trying to figure out how to establish central bank liquidity swap lines during a financial crisis. There would be two reasons we'd have nothing to eat.

In Europe, governments are being run by a coalition of populists from the far left and far right. In Italy, the Five Star Movement formed a government with the League; in Greece, Syriza aligned with Independent Greeks. In France, the left and right jointly protested gas taxes to reduce carbon emissions by burning cars in Paris while they wore yellow vests, because the French like to stay safe in traffic even when rioting.

These groups have a thousand differences but one thing in common: a hatred of the Intellectual Elite.

If the far left and far right are combining their navies, conservative and liberal members of the Intellectual Elite have to team up, too. Likely in a conference room at a resort hotel.

It turns out it's already happening. And one of the main participants is the person Tucker Carlson accused of leading the ship of elite fools off a cliff.

PART V

Saving the Elite

If you can keep your head when all about you
Are losing theirs and blaming it on you,
If you can trust yourself when all men doubt
you,
But make allowance for their doubting too;
If you can wait and not be tired by waiting,
Or being lied about, don't deal in lies,
Or being hated, don't give way to hating,
And yet don't look too good, nor talk too
wise:

—Rudyard Kipling, "If—", 1910

CHAPTER 20

The Meeting of the Concerned

I trust Bill Kristol. Not his political opinions, which are insane. The guy wants to bomb Iran. No, I trust Bill Kristol's commitment to Intellectual Elitism. He is the very model of a modern major elite: soft-spoken and chipper, with a default half smile that implies he's looking at a world as if it were a beautiful painting that's not quite centered on the wall. There are no photos from any period of Bill Kristol's life where he does not look old. He always responds to my requests for quotes, an act of noblesse oblige to make my humor columns a little less dumb.

Bill, of course, does not own a boat. Though he did board one each year for the cruise organized by the conservative magazine he cofounded, the *Weekly Standard*. On the 2014 voyage, Bill kept an online diary that includes an entry that alights my Intellectual Elite heart. At the ship's stop at St. Kitts and Nevis, Bill didn't indulge in swimming or snorkeling like the other passengers, writing: "Bah to such pleasure-seeking!" He did not investigate the nation's "citizenship by investment" opportunity that my friend Neil Strauss suggested. Bill visited the museum of early-nineteenth-century British war genius Lord Nelson, a museum so tiny and uninteresting that he had to get someone to unlock it for him.

Bill is a second-generation Intellectual Elite. His father, Irving Kristol, was a member of a group of writers redundantly called the New York Intellectuals. The *Daily Telegraph* called him "perhaps the most consequential public intellectual of the latter half of the 20th century." He was awarded the Medal of Freedom and played in a weekly poker game with Supreme Court justices Antonin Scalia and William Rehnquist. In a 1977 essay, Irving wrote: "It would never have occurred to us to denounce anyone or anything as 'elitist.' The elite was us—the 'happy few' who had been chosen by History to guide our fellow creatures toward a secular redemption." Bill's mother, Gertrude Himmelfarb, is a former history professor who focused on Victorian England, which is the period of England that even the English find too England-y.

Bill spent more time at Harvard than John Harvard. He graduated magna cum laude in three years, got a PhD in history, and taught political philosophy there.

Harvard is where Bill met his wife, who later got a PhD in classical philology. Do you know how hard it is for a Republican to get a girlfriend at an Ivy League school, especially if he's only turned on by philologists, which I'm pretty sure are people who love giving oral sex? During their courtship, they got into opera, a hobby so elite it trumps when my college girlfriend and I got into playing bridge and making bad puns, such as that "trump" one.

After Harvard, Bill worked for Republican politicians, cofounded Republican think tanks, started a Republican magazine, wrote Republican columns for newspapers, and appeared as a Republican on television news shows. So when the Boat Elite came to take his Republican Party from the Intellectual Elite, he fought to beat them back. When, despite his best efforts, Trump won the Republican nomination, he had to choose between the two biggest parts of his identity, the Intellectual Elite and the Republican. He didn't consider it much of a choice. He declared civil war, trying desperately to draft another Republican to run as a third-party candidate in the 2016 election against his own party. Trump retaliated by nicknaming him "Dummy Bill Kristol."

This Republican civil war is why Tucker put Bill in the bow of the USS *Intellectual Elitism*. But the beef between the philosopher king of the Republican Boat Elite and the philosopher king of the Republican Intellectual Elite is also personal. Tucker worked for Bill for six years as a star writer at the *Weekly Standard* and considered him his mentor. "I haven't really had, in my whole life, a falling out with anyone. Bill Kristol is the only person I liked in 1995 who I don't like now. I think he's very, very dishonest in the deepest sense," Tucker told me. "He's a pretty sinister person." Though he wouldn't elaborate, he did repeat "sinister" a few times, which made me think it was something more personal than wanting to bomb Iran, though that is pretty sinister.

The other reason Tucker put Bill in the front of that ship is that he does represent the failures of the Intellectual Elite. Whatever movie Bill Kristol is watching is worse at predicting the future than *Escape from New York* was. Bill was gung-ho on the Iraq War, saying it was "pop psychology" that the Sunnis and Shiites in the country didn't get along. On the 2007 *Weekly Standard* cruise to Alaska, Bill grabbed a lunch at the governor's mansion, where the newly elected Sarah Palin served halibut cheeks and impressed him so much with her knowledge that when Bill served as John McCain's foreign policy adviser, he suggested he pick her as his vice-presidential candidate. As Trump said about Bill during a rally: "Why do you keep putting a guy on television that's been proven to be wrong for so many years?" Yes, Trump is employing the Meteorologist Fallacy™ because Bill made many predictions over many decades, but if Bill Kristol were a meteorologist you could make a montage of him half smiling in sunglasses and a bathing suit before being swept away by hurricanes.

Still, Bill's commitment to Intellectual Elitism über alles makes him the perfect Founding Father of the new political party that I want to create. In the Intellectual Elite party, conservatives will sit at a table with liberals, saying grace over meals of cold-pressed juice. We'd put aside our petty disagreements about how much communism to dip in our capitalism and focus on saving the Pax Europa built after World War II via alliances, free trade, science, a free press, and political debates in which no one nicknames their opponent Dummy.

Bill is already starting to work on this, in exactly the way I hoped he would: he's joined a secretive, elitist organization that works to save the Intellectual Elite. Even better, he is a member of two secretive, elitist organizations that do this. Patriots and Pragmatists consists of a mix of about fifty Republicans and Democrats who meet a few times a year. One conference was held at Sausalito's Cavallo Point, a resort built on a former army base that has rooms that were former officers's residences and a spa offering "energy work," thereby pleasing and annoying both left and right. The group has yet to talk about forming a new political party, instead focusing on ways to tout democratic ideals. This sounds lazy to me. I fear they spend too much time in conference rooms and not enough time doing energy work.

Nevertheless, I like this group. Especially its name. If a power-mad senator asks if you are, or have ever been, a member of Patriots and Pragmatists, you can proudly say yes. Though to be extra safe, I would have called it Patriots, Pragmatists, and Puppies. Still, the key part is *patriots*, a word which I've been thinking about since a smiley woman introduced herself after services at the First Baptist Church of Miami, Texas. Elaine McDowell, mother of Zachary, grandmother of Rifle, and one day, I'm guessing, great-grandmother of Kachow!, pumped my hand and, in a cheery voice reserved for queries about the weather, asked a question no one had ever posed to me: "What do you think about flag burning?"

I informed her that I was not personally into flag burning. This didn't seem to satisfy her, so I told Elaine that I'd been thinking a lot about the flag lately. When I was a kid, Democrats thought of the flag as a positive symbol of America like the bald eagle, the Statue of Liberty, Uncle Sam, the Liberty Bell, or money. But in the last decade the flag became associated with nationalism. Minorities see it as a warning sign. It is one color away from the Confederate flag on the political spectrum, and zero colors away on the color spectrum. Since the Trump election, real estate agents in my neighborhood no longer advertise by planting flags on our lawns on the Fourth of July. No house near me flies a flag. A guy who lives in Brooklyn told me his son won't wear his American flag bathing suit anymore lest people think he's a member of the alt-right. This is a kid so fearless he hadn't cared what people thought of his horrible fashion sense.

I want to reclaim patriotism from the nationalists. Devotion to the ideals of our country is too powerful to cede. I want to do what Jill Sobule did at my neighbor Stephanie's party when she got us to sing a version of Lee Greenwood's "God Bless the USA" that she altered with more progressive lyrics. Abbie Hoffman called this idea "capturing the flag" when he proudly wore an American flag as a long-sleeve shirt, or when Medgar Evers got civil rights protestors to carry American flags as they marched in Mississippi. There's a bracket on a beam in the front of my house that, after an embarrassing number of years of staring at it in confusion, someone explained is for holding a flag. I went online to buy an American flag but couldn't muster enough patriotism to withstand the comments I knew my neighbors would make. A California state flag now waves from our house. The Bear Flag is my first step toward patriotism, though I fear it is a proclamation of rebellion, the liberal Confederate flag. Part of the reason I fear this is because the flag has one star, which represents California being its own country, as do the words CALIFORNIA REPUBLIC on the bottom. And the bear is walking to the left, like a Russian commie bear. Plus, I'm pretty sure if you look closely at the grass below its feet, you'll see that the bear is defecating on America.

Elaine seemed glad that I wasn't burning the flag and instead boring her about it with a lot of words, like liberals do with everything. We said goodbye and I went to my car, when, to my surprise, she ran after me. I was confused. Did she want my thoughts on Ferdinand de Saussure's theory on the arbitrary connection between signifier and signified?

Elaine wanted to know what I thought of NFL quarterback Colin Kaepernick kneeling during the national anthem to protest police officers shooting black people. Specifically, she wanted to know if I thought his message would have been much more effective if he coupled it by volunteering to help at-risk black kids. I said that he did volunteer and give money to those causes, but his main goal was to bring attention to racism. She countered, oh-so-politely, that if he helped those kids more, they wouldn't be getting pulled over by the cops in the first place. I suggested that perhaps Kaepernick failed to deliver his message, which is that those kids are getting pulled over unjustly. "Well," she said in a chipper voice, "they had to do something wrong." Which is what Jodye and Mark Tarpley had said to me, and I still didn't have an answer that wasn't classist.

Political disagreements have split ownership of "The Star-Spangled Banner" the same way they have with the American flag. It's strange how quickly symbols shift. I have a photo of my dad's bar mitzvah in 1953, and the cantor is startling looking; he may be the last person to keep his once friendly (Oliver Hardy! Charlie Chaplin! Walt Disney!) toothbrush mustache after Hitler poisoned it. I want Patriots and Pragmatists to restore American symbols to all of us, largely so I can take down this ridiculous Bear Flag.

In case Patriots and Pragmatists fails, the second secretive, elitist organization that works to save the Intellectual Elite that Bill belongs to has a more direct plan: to expunge the Boat Elite from the Republican Party. This organization also has a great name: the Meeting of the Concerned. Since the 2016 election, Bill and more than one hundred other Intellectual Elite Republicans meet every other week to figure out how to regain control of their party. "Concerned is a euphemism. It's the Meeting of the Freaked Out," says member Brink Lindsey. To my chagrin, they do not drink brandy in a wood-paneled office like the original Book of the Month Club judges. "The aesthetics match the mood. We have a windowless conference room with various breakfast items," says Brink about the basement offices of the Niskanen Center, a libertarian think tank. I have never heard a term as sad as "various breakfast items." Even the Holiday Inn calls them "hot and fresh fare."

I am not allowed to attend the Meeting of the Concerned since some members are worried that I'll reveal their names and Boat Elite Republicans will expunge them from the party, thereby decreasing their power to change it. The group is so secretive that CNN has never covered it despite the fact that their meetings are in the same building as CNN's DC headquarters.

So I reproduced a meeting. I found out who the members were, called them while I ate a tiny muffin and cereal from one of those single-serving boxes you can pour milk into, and started the conversation by saying, "Can you believe what Trump did today?"

The first thing I learned in my pretend basement conference room was that members of the Meeting of the Concerned do not agree on how to handle populists. The two competing philosophies are *change* and *fight*. These are the ones that Tucker Carlson and his daughter argued about: Is it better for the Intellectual Elite to study the populists' criticisms and adjust our policies, or to shout at them for being racist idiots? This will be the toughest debate within the new left-and-right Intellectual Elite party, causing more friction than our positions on taxes, gun control, abortion, or entitlement spending.

Every one of my liberal friends has chosen *fight*. They cheered the DC restaurant that kicked out Sarah Huckabee Sanders for working as Trump's press secretary. This began a rash of liberals accosting Republicans at restaurants. Tucker Carlson said he doesn't go out to restaurants in DC anymore other than the Palm steakhouse, since "having someone scream, 'Fuck you!' at a restaurant, it just wrecks your meal." Liberals on Twitter responded that people who bash the elite don't deserve to eat at elite restaurants; Bill Prady, the co-creator of the sitcom *The Big Bang Theory*, suggested that Tucker dine where he belongs, at the KKKFC. The Intellectual Elite don't realize we're on the verge of being circulated, and once we are, so will our organic, small-plate, farm-to-table, vegetable-forward restaurants. Once the Boat Elite take over, it's all steakhouses with sixty-four-ounce bottles of ketchup on every table.

The Intellectual Elite didn't used to embrace *fight*. Michelle Obama's directive from her 2016 Democratic convention speech was "When they go low, we go high." But two years later, former Obama attorney general Eric Holder told a crowd, "When they go low, we kick them." Democratic representative Maxine Waters, one of the eight people on Tucker's book cover, held a rally in Los Angeles that was 10 miles from my house and 1.8 miles from a Whole Foods, in which she said, "If you see anybody from that Cabinet in a restaurant, in a department store, at a gasoline station, you get out and you create a crowd and you push back on them and you tell them they're not welcome anymore, anywhere." When protestors went to the Michelin-starred Fiola to harass Senator Ted Cruz until he left, my college friend Michael Green, a pacifist screenwriter, tweeted, "He should never leave the house in peace again." This seemed, as Tucker had argued to his daughter, harassment unbefitting people with our education and comfortable lives. So I explained to Michael that I think it's wrong to punch Nazis, and that Martin Luther King Jr. and Mahatma Gandhi were clearly on the side of nonviolent protest. Michael's answer to me, on Twitter, was "See a Nazi punch a Nazi." The same week that Republican senator Mitch McConnell and his wife, Transportation Secretary Elaine Chao, were harassed at a restaurant in their hometown in Kentucky, Michael tweeted, "Fuck civility!" He followed that with this explanation: "When your opponents are liars and cheats and thieves who celebrate violence be as rude as you fucking want," which I assume he typed before ripping his T-shirt down the center with both hands. A couple of months after I spoke to Tucker Carlson, about twenty people showed up at his house at night, chanting, "Tucker Carlson, we will fight! We know where you sleep at night!" and spray painted an anarchist symbol in his driveway.

These attacks seem like the oppressed fighting back against their oppressors, but they're actually skirmishes in the war between the Intellectual and Boat Elite. The restaurant yellers aren't ethnic minorities. This is all rich-white-on-rich-white violence. More than 90 percent of whites with postgraduate degrees who voted for Hillary Clinton believe it's "racist for a white person to want less immigration to help maintain the white share of the population," while only 45 percent of minority voters feel that way. More than 80 percent of white people who voted for Hillary Clinton think diversity makes America stronger, while only 54 percent of black voters agree. A 2018 survey by More in Common, an international group that's trying to help form centrist anti-populist parties, divided voters into seven groups and found that "progressive activists" (the Intellectual Elite minus the ones who are Republican) make up only 8 percent of the United States. We are twice as likely as the average American to make more than $100,000 a year, three times more likely to have gone to grad school, and way more likely to be white. Only 3 percent of progressive activists are black. Progressive activists are me and my friends. Only 1 percent of progressive activists say the American flag makes them feel "extremely good," while 80 percent of Elaine McDowell's corresponding group all the way to the right, the "devoted conservatives," do. Likewise, 1 percent of my people are against requiring professional athletes to stand during the national anthem, while 95 percent of hers are for it. The point is that if Elaine McDowell were a professional poll question writer, she'd make enough money to put Kachow! through college.

My group is the one most scared about the Boat Elite coming to power because we have the most to lose. We are the elite they are digging a graveyard for. Being white, successful, educated, and panicked about being circulated doesn't make us wrong about the fact that civilization is imperiled. But it does make us extra angry.

Fear is not a good reason to surrender to the gut instict to fight. The most important thing we elite can do is act elite. If we sacrifice our commitment to civility, discourse, reason, inclusion, and cooperation—if we bully people for their beliefs—we have abandoned our values for theirs. We will become Boat Elite. In 1945 Pauli Murray, the civil rights activist and cofounder of the National Organization for Women, wrote:

> I do not intend to destroy segregation by physical force. I intend to destroy segregation by positive and embracing methods. When my brothers try to draw a circle to exclude me, I shall draw a larger circle to include them. Where they speak out for the privileges of a puny group, I shall shout for the rights of all mankind.

Bill Kristol is also against *fight*. That's partly because he's nonconfrontational outside of his obsession with bombing countries. When we talked about Tucker Carlson's book cover, Bill didn't say that Tucker is sinister. He said he was flattered to be leading the ship and excited to discover that Mark Zuckerberg takes instructions from him.

But it's mostly because Bill believes in the Intellectual Elite principles he learned from his parents and from Harvard. He believes in studying the evidence and adjusting accordingly. He believes in change.

He doesn't entirely disagree with Tucker's assault on the Intellectual Elite. He admits that the Iraq War went disastrously, Sarah Palin wasn't fit to be vice president of St. Kitts and Nevis, and economists failed to prevent the Great Recession. The Intellectual Elite are vulnerable to these kinds of errors because of our hubris, and we should correct for it. "In the 1930s and '40s, intellectuals were more susceptible to communism than most people. There's an element of skepticism of experts—healthy common sense, the guy who worked his way up—that's not unhealthy in a democracy or in everyday life. That hardheaded skepticism is different than a populist anger at anyone who says things are more complicated than you might think," he says. I think Bill might have a point until he references my least favorite anti-elitist quote. It's populist pablum from one of the greatest populist elites in history, William F. Buckley Jr., the Skull and Bones Yalie with the Mid-Atlantic accent who played the harpsichord and hosted a show on PBS. Despite all of this, he said, "I should sooner live in a society governed by the first 2,000 names in the Boston telephone directory than in a society governed by the 2,000 faculty members of Harvard University." It would indeed be a wicked pissah society where disagreements were settled via a drinking contest in which each time someone looks up from his beer, you punch him in the throat.

Meeting of the Concerned member Geoffrey Kabaservice is also for *change*. The director of political studies at Niskanen, Geoffrey is undeniably a member of the Intellectual Elite. He got both his bachelor's degree and PhD in history from Yale. His blond hair swoops down over his face twice as far as someone's with only one Yale degree. "Sometimes deference to elites is not a good idea. Elites certainly screwed up in the run-up to the financial crisis and deserve a lot of the blowback they receieved," he says. "The solution is going to come from elites listening and being more receptive than they have in the past."

Another Concerned member, Niskanen's vice president for policy Brink Lindsey (Princeton; Harvard Law) also supports *change*. He came up with the same analogy that Tucker did to describe the Intellectual Elite's reaction to Trump's election: We blamed the messenger instead of receiving the message. He suggests we restore faith in the Intellectual Elite through basic, Eric Garcetti–style pothole improvements, such as eliminating red tape concerning zoning, licensing, and patent law that hampers small businesses. He coauthored *The Captured Economy: How the Powerful Enrich Themselves, Slow Down Growth, and Increase Inequality*, which is a stirring indictment of how the powerful enrich themselves, slow down growth, and increase inequality.

I'm as fired up about regulatory capture as the next guy as long as the next guy isn't Brink Lindsey, but it's hard for me to join *change*. In order to change your ideas, you must be presented with better ones.

And the populists' ideas are awful: tariffs, closed borders, slashed interest rates, unregulated use of fossil fuels, conspiracy theories, autocracy. The majority can be wrong. If they weren't, society would never have chosen a tiny Intellectual Elite to run things. The majority was wrong about allowing slavery, it was wrong about empowering Nazis, it was wrong about sending Japanese-Americans to internment camps, it was wrong about every natural phenomenon being caused by Greek gods. History has proven the majority wrong about music, films, hairstyles, and my first book, which did not sell well.

Neither *fight* nor *change* seemed like a great solution. Plus, they both sounded like a lot of work. Luckily, one of the members of the Meeting of the Concerned came up with a third way.

CHAPTER 21

I Said, "Good Day, Sir!"

om Nichols is naturally a *fight* kind of guy. He grew up working class in Massachusetts, smokes cigars, teaches at the Naval War College, and took in a feral cat. He is a man so fearless that he has a goatee despite the fact that it is 2019. When he was about to walk on the *Jeopardy!* stage, a fellow contestant said to him in the backstage darkness, "You don't want to beat me in front of my eight-year-old daughter, do you?" To which Tom icily responded, "You don't want to beat me in front of my new wife, do you? Your daughter will always love you, but my wife will leave me." He won five days in a row before being mandatorily retired due to the show's old, weak-kneed rules.

Tom is the author of *The Death of Expertise*, which

is a lot like this book only far better, which is why I waited to tell you about it until you were nearly done with this one. He believes the elites' biggest failure was listening to the complaints of the masses. "When I gave talks around the county people would say, 'We have to do something because Washington doesn't listen to us.' I would get really mad and say, 'Washington listens to you too much. It gives you what you keep asking for. And the problem is what you're asking for is internally contradictory and changes every few years. Do you want a national health care system or expanded Medicare? You answer, "We want both and lower taxes." No one in Washington says, "You can't have that." They say, "Yes sir! We'll go and do it!"'" Tom says. When friends from his hometown complain that Americans don't make televisions anymore, Tom counters that they each want three flat screens, which on their income means they have to be made in a country with cheap labor. "Their answer is always, 'Why don't the companies take less money?' They want these elites running corporations to be selfless socialists but they also want to vote against selfless socialists," he says, exasperated.

Likewise, when people complain that television news is sensationalist, he tells them that no one today will watch the hour-long specials on national defense that CBS News ran in the 1980s. He doesn't even have to reach back thirty years to make this point. When people blame the mainstream media for not covering some serious subject, I respond by asking if they read the *Economist* or watch the BBC. I do this mostly to be a dick, since I don't read the *Economist* or watch the BBC. But I'm also making a point: when people say "mainstream news" they mean cable news, and in order to stay mainstream those channels must cover the dumb crap people are interested in. Otherwise, they stop being mainstream, and people will make that same complaint about the next mainstream news source that takes their place. This is how you get a History Channel with shows about ghosts and aliens.

Tom blames homeowners for the mortgage crisis. "You told your public official, 'Change these regulations.' Then you walked into a bank and bought a house you couldn't afford. If there weren't bad mortgages there wouldn't have been stupid instruments to make money off of bad mortgages," he says. I agree. Mortgage contracts have numbers in huge fonts stating how much money you'll owe each month, whether that will change, and how much you'll pay in total over the course of the loan. You have to sign next to each of those numbers. I am aware that what I wrote might cause the California authorities to confiscate my Bear Flag.

Tom dismisses Tucker's theory that this populist wave was caused by wealth inequality and that "it's so much worse than the Depression." Of course things were worse during the Great Depression. They were even worse in the late 1970s. "I graduated high school in 1979, the most nihilistic year there was. Every valedictorian in 1979 in America gave a commencement speech that began 'Whatever.' Nixon, Vietnam, stagflation, Jimmy Carter, whatever. We were like, 'Nothing works. Everything is corrupt,'" he says. Punk music was huge then, not now. You can't rage against the machine when you're tripping on molly at an electronic dance festival.

Tom is so against *change* that he announced on Twitter that he's no longer listening to populist whining:

> It's not that I disagree about policy with Trump supporters. It's that I know they don't give a shit about policy.... Most of them are only interested in Trump as a vehicle of social disruption. Trump's smarter enablers see him as an equalizer, a way to put them on an equal footing with "elites"—oh, that word—who they think look down on them. Thing is, the elites *do* look down on them. For good reason. Most of Trump's sycophants are second raters, at best. For them, Trump is their shot.... This is their one chance to grab the car keys and throw a kegger before Mom and Dad get back home.

Trump is a giant middle finger. He's that long line of political cocaine Scott Adams snorted. You can't argue about the folly of replicating the Smoot-Hawley Tariff Act with a coked-up dude giving you the finger.

Geoffrey Kabaservice, the swoopy haired Concerned member, is frustrated by seeing politicians host town hall meetings that devolve into mob shouting. "Having respect for Congress as an institution should be part of a 'small c' conservative culture. You put your hand on your heart when you salute the flag, you wear a suit to church, and you wear a suit when you talk to someone from Congress," he says. "If you honestly thought you had a solution, would you come to a town hall unshaven in a T-shirt to talk to a member of Congress? I don't think these people believe this is how political change happens. They just want to shout and feel good."

Bill Kristol feels the same frustration. "The appeal to expertise doesn't work, obviously. The appeals to history and common sense don't work. Maybe modern liberal skepticism and rational argument has always been a little bit more tenuous than you think. People think, 'That kind of society doesn't do much for me and is kind of boring,'" he says. "I went to a couple of the Trump rallies in 2016 and there's a lot of 'This is a lot more fun than a boring political speech.' It's a combination of anger and entertainment." Henry Adams came to the same conclusion: "The world never loved perfect poise. What the world does love is commonly absence of poise, for it has to be amused. Napoleans and Andrew Jacksons amuse it, but it is not amused by perfect balance." From 2015 to 2019, one of the most popular television shows in Ukraine was

Servant of the People, a sitcom about a public school teacher whose students secretly videotape him ranting about the corrupt elites. "It's always the lesser of two assholes, and it's been this way for twenty-five years," he says. "If I could have one week in office, if such a thing were possible, I would show them! Fuck the motorcades! Fuck the perks! Fuck the weekend chalets!" The kids post it on YouTube, where it becomes so popular that he's elected president. In 2018, the star of *Servant of the People* formed a party called Servant of the People and ran for president by avoiding interviews, debates, and policy announcements, instead posting Instagram videos about the corrupt elite. In place of speeches at rallies, he charged tickets to giant comedy shows. On April 21, 2019, he won the presidency with more than 73 percent of the vote. The people of Ukraine, a country mired in economic troubles and at war with Russia, were so interested in being entertained, they were willing to be amused to death.

The urge to play a joke on the elite is so strong that even the Intellectual Elite are susceptible. In 1992, Stanford's star football player, future NFL Pro Bowler Glyn Milburn, and I, a *Stanford Daily* humor columnist, ran on a slate for the copresidency of the student government against a serious group of experienced students. We both lost to a third party called I Prefer Not to Have a Council of Presidents, whose entire platform consisted of vowing not to serve. Let's just say that the emergency call boxes Glyn and I promised to install around campus wouldn't come for another decade, which was particularly dumb since everyone had a cell phone by then.

Instead of fight or change, Tom's strategy for the Intellectual Elite is to disengage. When someone with an inane belief baits you into a debate, don't legitimize them by participating. In a speech to the National Academy of Sciences—a group I'm pretty sure I was president of my senior year of high school—Tom told them to stop talking to morons who seek attention by challenging them. "If someone walks up to you and says the earth is flat, you say, 'Let's explore that together.' Stop saying that! Say, 'I'm an astrophysicist,'" he said. The speech didn't go over well. "They said, 'People don't like being condescended to.' Well, they don't like being patronized, either. I think people are tired of elites saying, 'I hear you.' Say, 'Vaccinate your fucking kids. I'm not having this conversation with you.'" It's what Dr. Klein did to Danielle in their improv skit.

If, as Tucker says, good leadership is like good parenting, then Tom's strategy makes sense. When your kid throws a tantrum, you don't tantrum back. They want to bait you into yelling at them so they can transfer some of their frustration onto you. They need to learn to control their selfish rage. You don't negotiate with children, terrorists, or populists.

I already use Tom's technique. In fact, I've successfully used it in exactly the situation he mentioned: to convince people to vaccinate their kids. That people was my wife. Shortly after Laszlo was born in 2009, Cassandra bought two thirty-dollar tickets so we could listen to an antivaccination doctor. I sat gobsmacked as Dr. Lauren Feder told us that contracting whooping cough is awesome since it protects kids from asthma. Measles kept away eczema, and only 1 percent of babies who got polio became paralyzed. I tried to stay calm and act like I, too, longed for a past where pockmarked polio children frolic in woods while coughing up their lungs. But eventually I raised my hand and asked Dr. Feder if she thought putting off Laszlo's hepatitis B vaccine for a while—as Cassandra suggested, to space out his exposure to something or increase his exposure to something else—would pose a problem if some hep-B kid bit him on the playground.

"You go with what feels right," Dr. Feder told me.

I was not going to be outpatronized. I told her I was less interested in feelings than science.

"I don't see hep B in my practice very often," she said. "I see hep B–vaccine side effects. Which is multiple sclerosis. I respond to what I see."

Unfortunately, so do I, and I saw red. She was answering me from her "own immediate experience," which David Foster Wallace had warned against, instead of "reading the research," which is what they teach in medical school. I asked Dr. Feder directly if hep B can be transmitted through saliva, and she responded that a biting child was an improbable scenario. I deeply considered telling Laszlo, who was in my lap, to crawl onstage and, this one time, bite someone. Instead, I kept my cool and asked my question a third time, which, admittedly, isn't really keeping your cool.

"Can hep B be transmitted through saliva?" I asked.

"I don't go there," she responded.

Desperate to be at this place where Dr. Feder doesn't go, I walked to my car.

A few months after we talk, Tom quits the Republican Party after nearly forty years of membership. Two months after that, Trump-loving billionaire Philip Anschutz—who owns a cruise line of yachts—shut down the *Weekly Standard* after twenty-three years of publication, thereby also ending the magazine's annual cruise and severing Bill Kristol's only connection to boating. Tom and Bill were both available for our new party.

I was feeling good about our new party's strategy of disengaging. It was classy but self-righteous. It was indisputably elitist. Our party's motto will be "I said, 'Good day, sir.'"

Unfortunately, someone had a plan to engage me. And he'd been working on it for more than a year.

CHAPTER 22

The Love Dare

I was wrong. The people of Miami, Texas, did not forget me. They have been thinking about me more than I've been thinking about them, which is amazing because I'm writing a book about them. Ten months since I last saw her, Dee Ann Burkholder, my host from the Cowboys and Roses, sends me a Facebook message:

> At church tonight Jerry Wilmoth wanted me to ask you if you wanted to meet somewhere with him & Marian & Diane & Monty & kids on June 11th or 12th because they will all be in your neighborhood??! We all love you & think about you all the time!! Your visit here made us all happy & it was a blast!!! ♥ ♥ ☺ ☺ ☺ ☺ Keep in touch & always remember you have lots of friends in the big old town of Miami Texas!!!!

I am delighted that Jerry is coming. I'm even more delighted that I'm delighted that Jerry is coming. When he told me back in Miami that he might be visiting Los Angeles, I feared my elitism would make me stop caring about Jerry once I didn't need him. But I can't wait to see him and his wife, Marian, and Diane and Monty and kids, even though I don't know who Diane and Monty and kids are. I'm excited to hear about what's going on in Miami. I'm a way better person than I gave myself credit for. Not two-hearts, four-happy-faces, and ten-exclamation-points nice, but better than I feared.

Jerry calls me from his flip phone and asks me to pick a hamburger restaurant to meet him, his wife, his sister, Diane, her husband, Monty, and their three kids. They all love to go around the country trying the best burgers, which seems normal until I remember that they live in a town whose only restaurant is run by a cook who can make only two things well, and one of them is a hamburger. Jerry might as well have asked me to find the best store in Los Angeles that sells crap hoarded by the owner's dad.

I've barely gotten to find out anything about Miami when Jerry tells me that he sees the pastor from the First Baptist Church driving by his house and puts him on the phone with me. This seems a little weird, since I only said one sentence to the pastor while I was in Miami. Maybe Jerry is doing one of those old-guy things where they hate talking on the phone so they hand it off to whoever is nearby even if it requires chasing passing pickup trucks. Then I realize: the pastor must have found out about the stolen Sonic ice. He threatened to press charges against everyone on Baptist Row and they all blamed the Jew. The pastor is going to rain fire and brimstone on me, which I find out isn't as bad as I thought when I look up the word *brimstone* and find out it is sulfur. So like fire and bad smells, which doesn't sound as bad. Though it is a poetic punishment for stealing ice.

That is not what the pastor wants to discuss. Unlike at church services, where he constructed paper hats, the pastor goes straight to preaching. "Remember the Lord loves you and Jesus loves you and He died for you," he says.

"Thank you," I say, which I don't think is the right response. Maybe "You too!" would have been better. Or "I feel badly about that." I'm also confused as to why he said this to me. Maybe "Remember the Lord loves you and Jesus loves you and He died for you" is what preachers assume you want them to say when you shove a phone in their face, like the way Mr. T would yell, "I pity the fool!"

Before I can figure it out, Jerry gets back on the phone and tells me that every week since I left Miami, the pastor leads the church in a prayer for me. I figure he means that figuratively, like they pray for all living beings everywhere. No, Jerry explains, they pray for *me*. The church hands a photocopied Prayer Requests list to each member of the congregation, and I've been on every one since I left. It's not even a long list. There are about twelve other people on it with me, depending on who is sick at the time. The only other entries who have made the prayer list every single week have been "Our Nation & President," "Fire Dept., EMS, Sheriff," "Our US Troops," "Our School & Students," "Voice of Hope Ministry," and one other woman. Her name is not familiar, but I'm guessing she either has cancer or stopped in Miami for a few hours and offhandedly questioned the historical accuracy of Noah's ark.

While I feel guilty about causing so much concern that I was on a prayer list, I do like the publicity. Especially because *Time* magazine, former giant of the middlebrow, is under financial duress and, after nearly twenty years, eliminated my column. "You may not be in print in *Time* magazine anymore, but you're in print at the First Baptist Church of Miami," Jerry says.

"That doesn't pay as well in the short term," I say.

"But in the long term it pays off much more," he assures me. I'd missed bantering with my Miami friends about my eternal damnation.

I show up early at Cassell's Hamburgers and immediately regret my choice of restaurant. Sure, it looks like a diner, with counter service and flimsy wooden tables, but the $11.75 cheeseburger (fries not included) is going to come off as elitist. The $12.50 truffle fries definitely will. Plus, it's packed with tattooed hipsters of every race, sexuality, and gender.

Jerry walks in, with his beard and glasses and baseball cap, like I remember him. The restaurant does not throw him off. I feared he'd seem smaller and awkward in L.A., the way I must have in Miami, but he does not. Jerry knows who he is and that doesn't change depending on location or company. I, meanwhile, am a new person in every situation, shape shifting into my best guess of what people will like.

Jerry is excited about his burger, especially because he hasn't had one at the Rafter B Café in a while. The place closed down when Sam Bowers, the chef who waved a spatula while telling people to get the hell out, had a relapse and started drinking again. I suspected this when I saw his name on and off the church's weekly Prayer Requests list. Sam went to rehab, and he and his sister sold the café. I thought things didn't change in Miami, but they do. I should have known that after seeing those reversed before-and-after photos at the museum showing downtown empty today and studded with two drugstores, two grocery stores, a hat shop, two doctors' offices, a hotel, and three gas stations decades ago.

As we eat, Jerry's brother-in-law Monty makes a joke about feeling comfortable here after seeing a Trump sticker on a minivan when they were parking down the street. I do not smile or laugh. I am disengaging. Then all three adults tell me they're disappointed that Congress couldn't pass a farm bill because liberals wouldn't accept tightened work requirements for food stamp recipients. I will not be baited into this argument, either.

After we finish, I ask for the check, but the server tells me Jerry slipped her his credit card when he went to the bathroom. He'd hosted me both at the Rafter B and my hometown. He also brought me a gift.

I reach inside the red paper bag and pull out a book called *The Case for Christ*. He's also included a film called *The Case for Christ*, a film called *Fireproof*, and a three-film set that includes another copy of *The Case for Christ*. I immediately grasp that the most important of these is *The Case for Christ*. Jerry told me about the book when I was in Miami because it was written by a guy who used to be an atheist reporter like I am. I'm touched that Jerry cares so much about my soul that he wants to save it. But the disengager in me knows Jerry's desire is a bit selfish. And not only because if he got to heaven and I wasn't there it technically wouldn't be heaven but a place where everyone kept saying, "This is nice and all, but I wish Joel Stein were here," not wholly unlike the experience of reading *Time* magazine. It's also selfish because Jerry wants to increase his tribe in order to shape the world in his image. Or, more accurately, His image.

The Intellectual Elite aren't handing Trump voters bags of Jonathan Franzen novels. We're not into recruiting. This is partly because increasing our membership would, by definition, make us less elite. This is why we keep our organizations secretive, our college acceptance rates below 10 percent, and our literature too challenging for Tucker Carlson. But it's also because we have been disengaging for a while. Back in the Reader's Digest Condensed Books days, we sent millions of bags of literary novels.

Jerry sees that I'm overwhelmed by the contents of the bag. "No pressure," he says. "Other than your soul going to hell." He says he's going to call me every month to see how I'm progressing in my studies. I tell him that seems a little intense, since my book editor isn't checking up on me that often. He nods as if he understands. Then he says he'll call every six weeks.

The morning after my burgers with Jerry, I'm at a breakfast meeting at the 101 Coffee Shop with a college friend. As I'm telling him about my dinner with Jerry, a man puts his hand on my shoulder. It is not Jesus Christ. It is Jerry, which is nearly as weird. This is not the Rafter B. Los Angeles is a huge city and I rarely go out for breakfast, and even more rarely to this restaurant. The only thing more miraculous than running into Jerry here is that when he sees us, he does not mention that this must be proof that Jesus wants me to read *The Case for Christ*.

Five weeks and six days after he visited me in Los Angeles, Jerry calls. I don't answer. When he calls six weeks after that, I again ignore it. I don't need to have a conversation about how unlikely it is that a former *Chicago Tribune* editor proved the Messiah's existence and didn't even win a Pulitzer. Also, I haven't read any of the books or watched the movies.

Cassandra keeps asking me if she can throw the Bag of Conversion away, but I can't let her. It's not that I think I would go to hell for it. She'd be the one throwing it away. It's that disengaging is hard. It feels mean. That bag keeps staring at me. Jerry made a lot of effort. If *The Case for Christ* also came as a puppet show, he would have performed it for me.

One night, I coyly ask Cassandra if she'd like to watch a movie. When she asks which one, I tell her that I'd rather not reveal the title, what it's about, or who is in it.

"Is it triple X?" she asks.

"It is definitely not triple X," I say, thrown off by both the guess and the fact that she used a term for pornography no one currently alive has ever heard. I'm also discombobulated because I want to switch plans and see if she'll watch porn.

"Are you in this movie?" she asks.

"Just watch the first few minutes," I plead. I could see why the Baptist pastor had to resort to paper hats to get people to listen to the good word.

The Case for Christ seems like a hard sell, so I put on *Fireproof*, a film starring 1980s teen heartthrob Kirk Cameron. We watch the entire movie and I can, in complete honesty, say that it is a movie. *Fireproof* is written and directed by the author of a book called *The Love Dare*, and centers around a man who reads a book called *The Love Dare*. This is exactly how I think *In Defense of Elitism* should be developed as a film.

The Love Dare directs readers to perform a different, specific act of generosity for their spouses every day for forty days. This seems like solid advice. Though it ruins it if you scream "Love Dare!" every time you do anything at all for your wife, which is what I took away from the film. It was going to be particularly annoying for Cassandra on day thirty-two, which advises, "If at all possible, try to initiate sex with your husband or wife today.... Ask God to make this enjoyable for both of you as well as a path to greater intimacy." This seems like a bad call. I may not be a religious scholar, but I believe there are things that even an omnipotent deity responds to with, "Too much information." Also, asking God to make it enjoyable seems like a way of copping out of oral stuff.

The *Fireproof* scene that most surprises me is when Kirk Cameron's character confronts his greatest demons: watching pornography and wanting to buy a boat. Sure, these two things represent lust and greed, but a boat is a specific form of greed. A boat one. He has spent much of the movie sneaking online to look at pictures of boats and naked women, though we viewers only get to see the boats. Now he's vowed to end his coveting. I am liking this guy and his anti-boatism until he solves his problem in the most Boat Elite manner possible. He takes his computer, the Library of Alexandria of our times, the symbol of the Intellectual Elite, and smashes it with an aluminum bat.

I'm about to call Jerry the next day to tell him I completed the assignment, but when I put *Fireproof* back in the Bag of Conversion, I see those three *The Case for Christ*s staring at me like they are the wise men, or the holy trinity, or some other thing that comes in threes in the New Testament that I am about to learn.

I plow through a few chapters of *The Case for Christ* before realizing it is going to take me a long time to finish. So I sacrifice even more of my Intellectual Elite principles and watch the film adaptation. I highly recommend it if the only two movies you can watch are *The Case for Christ* and *Fireproof*. It tells the story of a guy who writes a book called *The Case for Christ*, which is an even better way to adapt *In Defense of Elitism* than the plot of *Fireproof*. The film features hard-boiled, 1980 Chicago newspapermen, one of whom is a balding editor of the religion section who says things like "This is where the chili meets the cheese, my friend." This tough talk spurs our young, hotshot, red-Camaro-driving, hard-drinking, atheist journalist hero to investigate the resurrection of Christ in order to prove God doesn't exist. He gets a huge whiteboard where he writes down facts, circles questions, and tapes photos like he's running a murder investigation of a 2,000-year-old cold case.

I do not know if any of the arguments in *The Case for Christ* are decent. So I call my friend Reza Aslan, a religious studies scholar who is on the board of trustees for the Chicago Theological Seminary, is a member of the Society of Biblical Literature, wrote *Zealot: The Life and Times of Jesus of Nazareth*, and went to an elite conference with me. "He is using the scripture as proof for belief, but the scripture is a text of belief. The tautology there makes your head swim. He's saying these believers said they believe something, and I believe it because believers said they believe it and that's proof," Reza says. "Sacred history is not history, dude. It's the equivalent of saying there's proof that George Washington never told a lie. Because he cut down a cherry tree and told people about it."

I am mad at myself for being suckered by Jerry out of disengagement. To put an end to this, I call him and leave a message. He calls back a few hours later, explaining that he was at a revival meeting. This surprised me since Jerry did not seem like he was out of vive. He told me the revival sermon was about "how you should never miss an opportunity to talk to someone about the Lord." When Jerry saw I'd called, he told the whole revival meeting, and now this group prayed for me, too. Plus, Jerry said that another round of prayers were coming my way at the revival meeting tomorrow so I might "feel something."

I am not going to let Jerry bait me. I tell him that the movies didn't convert me. I pull up the notes on my computer from my conversation with Reza, but before I can start to argue, Jerry says, "Every time we talk we don't have to talk about this. I consider you a friend." He invites my family to stay in his motor home on his trip to Colorado this summer to hunt and fish.

Jerry tells me that the Rafter B reopened with new

owners, who tried to elite up the joint, renaming it the Sage Matt Café. "She tried to do chicken lasagna and stuff like that," Jerry says. She even charged two dollars for a cup of coffee, but, facing the fury of Miami, lowered it back to one. "Now she's making normal stuff. It's got to be fried in grease for us to like it."

Things hadn't gone well for Sam Bowers, the former cook. Jerry knows when an alcoholic is at his bottom, so he took the highway patrol officer to Sam's house to try to scare him straight. It didn't work. Sam died at forty-three, of cirrhosis of the liver.

I promise Jerry that next time he calls, I won't ignore it. I'm giving up on disengaging. It's lazy to dismiss the populists as racist, uneducated yokels. It's lazy to not find out what the problems are in their towns.

Tom Nichols admits that there are some downsides to disengagement. Disdain is not a proven successful political tactic. People run for president; they don't stand-still-with-their-hands-folded-and-heads-turned-away for president. Nevertheless, Tom thinks the best long-term strategy is to stand aside with bandages and ointment while the consequences of populism settle in—Ow! Tariffs make stuff expensive! Ow! We need immigrants to grow our economy! Ow! White supremacists beat me with a bat!—until voters realize the Boat Elite need to go.

He's sure our country is strong enough to withstand this rope-a-dope strategy. "We can survive another Great Depression if that's what it takes to understand how stupid Trumpism is. We can survive a pandemic if people are too stupid to vaccinate their own kids. Maybe a disaster is the only way out of this," Tom says. "We can pretty much survive anything as long as it's not World War Three." This is the least inspiring speech I've ever heard. Then Tom adds, "I have a friend who says, 'If the masses really don't want elite rule, I live on five acres in Rhode Island, I'll put in a security system and a moat and wait them out. Because eventually they're going to want clean water.'"

Tom's argument makes sense. But I also know that if the Keystone Cops comedy of paramilitary errors on my Hollywood Hills block bothers me now, a moat will make my isolation intolerable. I know that while the populists will tire themselves out in the long run, the economist John Maynard Keynes said, "In the long run we are all dead. Economists set themselves too easy, too useless a task if in tempestuous seasons they can only tell us that when the storm is long past the ocean is flat again." I know that Reid Hoffman said to me, "You should always ask yourself, 'Could I be wrong? And how can I learn here?' If you don't do that, you're the person trying to force your beliefs on someone else. You're the violent person." I know that on the long list of advice I wrote to give my son someday is "If you have a choice between blaming others and taking re-sponsibility, go with the latter." And I know that I liked those people in Miami, Texas, an awful lot.

Reid was right. We need Humble Elitism. We don't

have a choice. We need whatever medicine will cure the disease that threatens to decimate the society we nurtured. For decades we had the luxury of going days without checking the news. We no longer do. Populism endangers not only peace and prosperity but also the essence of elitism by enraging us into a tribal battle fought with emotions and body count. It's a war we can't win. So while the populists are the ones with a poisonous prescription of parochialism, I want to make a plea solely to my fellow Intellectual Elite, largely because you're the only ones who make it to the end of a book.

In 1992, Vice President Dan Quayle gave a speech to the Southern Baptist Convention in Indianapolis under the advice of his chief of staff, the oft-wrong Bill Kristol, who undoubtedly regrets it. "We have two cultures: the cultural elite and the rest of us," Quayle said. "I wear their scorn as a badge of honor." It is hard to admit that the man who could not spell *potato* and thought it was likely that we could breathe on Mars understood something, but he did.

The fuel of populism is rage at those who claim higher status. To extinguish the populists' fire, we have to stop dismissing them as deplorable, racist, ignorant, unsophisticated, sexist, and I'm going to stop here in case someone tweets this sentence, which will impede my strategy. We have to bite our lips, feel their pain, and do that thing where you slowly nod while squinting. When Cassandra vents about an injustice she's experienced, I try to explain the other person's rationale so she can negotiate a solution. To which she says, "You're not on my team!" No one takes advice from someone who's not on their team. Especially when the other person's team is the New York Yankees.

I fail when I'm smug. The thing I've been most smug about is not listening to decades of people telling me I'm smug. I was so young when people started calling me smug that they used the word *precocious*, which means "smug child." My smugness is the least elite part of me. It's insecurity stemming from yearning to be in The Loop. It's tribal—a way to exclude others by drawing a circle around ourselves. It also fails our beloved scientific method because it almost never works. The only people who have ever been convinced by smugness are shoppers at Whole Foods.

We have to stop introducing ourselves by listing our jobs, our secret organizations, and what college we attended, which I am refraining from doing right here, which is not easy even though I know you can find out by flipping back to pages 7, 9, 15, 52, 113, 122, 124, 179, 211, or 247. We need to stop acting as if our electric cars, our organic food, and our fair-trade, single-origin coffee make us more evolved humans, when they simply make us poorer humans. We need to stop lecturing West Virginians about the obvious inanity of remaining in the coal industry when we are working in the book industry.

The truly elite people I know don't do these things.

When I asked a college professor at the college I went to if he had really read all the books that lined his house, he said that of course he hadn't. His wife later told me that of course he had.

Since I started this book, I've changed my mind about my superiority. It happened because I listened to others due to the fact that it's hard to talk when you're taking notes. By doing so I learned that gathering on a porch with your neighbors is better than sending texts. I've learned that the old quilts, the ones that went for comfort over pretty, are better. I've learned to entertain strangers. I've learned that even when other people's problems are minor injuries suffered in the name of progress, they're still real. And I've learned that your wife can remove your cross carved out of a book from your office, you can put it back, she can remove it, and you can put it back again, all without ever talking about it.

Humility is not much of an ask. Part of embracing facts, logic, and history is knowing that we will sometimes be wrong. Galileo was wrong about tides. Albert Einstein was wrong about quantum physics. I was wrong about smugness. The point is: I'm exactly like Galileo and Einstein. This smugness thing is going to be tough to overcome. But if anyone can do it, it's us. Seriously, this is not going to be easy.

Acknowledgments

I always wondered why books have acknowledgment sections. Then I was acknowledged in someone else's book and it all made sense to me. Based on that epiphany, I have put every acknowledgee in bold, to make scanning for your own name easier.

Unlike those who work in film, theater, and television, who can thank their collaborators on award shows if they create outstanding works, authors can thank people even if they wrote a mediocre book. And we can go on for as long as we want, without being cut off by soaring music.

Writing a book is so awful that I'm pretty sure Adolf Hitler chose the title *Mein Kampf* to refer to the struggle he had writing it. It is not something one can do alone, although I did. That's what being a true member of the elite is all about. Nevertheless, I am grateful for the following people:

Gretchen Young edited this book, which is her job as the editor of this book, so I don't know if that needs acknowledging. But she also risked her reputation to save this book, which originally was a crappy series of personal essays that were so bad I missed deadlines and then refused to publish the nominally finished product. She convinced her bosses to give me another chance with a new idea about elitism. When that effort was subpar as well, she gently told me so and bought me another six months to rewrite it. She is smart, funny, and so generous that she is willing to let one of her colleagues edit my next book.

My agent, **Suzanne Gluck**, negotiated with Gretchen to not give up on me, even though I'm sure Suzanne herself had given up on me.

I have never met, spoken to, or emailed with **Karen Thompson**, which I believe is her wise choice. She was this book's copy editor, a job she had to labor at even with the phrase "copy editor," which I thought was one word. She made sentences clearer, funnier, and correcter. Most of them. **Jeff Holt** handled production editing, which means he wanted me to stop fiddling around with changes so he could print the book. But he never said that to me. I suspect Jeff is the only person in the world who is afraid of me.

My dad, **Charlie Stein,** read every draft of every version of this book, always within forty-eight hours. It makes you strong when you know someone is so unfailingly present for you. He has read more books than anyone I know, and apparently that has taught him something. He loves me so much he didn't hold back in his criticism. Though he didn't need to repeat the same criticisms so many times. But he also didn't hold back on his praise. My mom, **Roz Leszczuk**, was also a very early reader, the kind who tells you how funny you are and that you shouldn't cut anything. Which is the kind of reader I hope you are. The two of them raised me with so much safety and encouragement that I grew up believing that people would be interested in reading three hundred pages of my thoughts.

When I was struggling with a final draft, *Vanity Fair* contributor **Nick Bilton**, the author of *Hatching Twitter* and *American Kingpin*, speed-read my book, invited me to his house for espressos, and told me how to build tension, add cliffhangers, and focus on characters. I would thank him by buying him more of the world's most elite soap that I used in his bathroom, Aesop Reverence Aromatique (bergamot rind, veviter root, and bits of finely milled pumice), but it is thirty-nine dollars a bottle.

Author **Neil Strauss** (*The Game*, *The Truth*) read an early rough draft of this book that I didn't know was an early rough draft. He used the Socratic method to teach me that a book isn't a series of articles, but one giant article. He then taught me how to structure a giant article. A few times.

One of the brave *Time* editors who handled my column, **Matt Vella**, read this book and suggested cuts, fixes, and a joke in his native French. I'm sure you all remember laughing on page 72 at "*très français*." That was pure Vella.

I was lucky to have worked for one of the best editors I will ever have when I was at my college newspaper. **Martha Brockenbrough**, author of the young adult book *Unpresidented: A Biography of Donald Trump*, read an early draft and loaded me up with comments questioning my white male privilege. She's also the founder of the Society for the Promotion of Good Grammar, so she fixed a lot of errors. Its amazing how many they're was. Her brilliant daughter, **Lucy Berliant**, got the **Garfield High School Latin Club** to translate the epigraph of this book, which Google Translate, who went to an inferior high school, botched. **Jamie Meyer**, a Latin and Greek high school teacher at Crossroads, perfected the translation.

I forgot what a good writer my college friend **Patty Kao** was since she's not a professional writer and does business stuff, but I remembered when she removed the plaque from my sentences. If you want to piss Patty off, use the word *since* when *because* would be better and do it 150 times.

Another person who edited me at *Time*, **Josh Tyrangiel**, who ran *Vice*'s nightly news show on HBO, read an early version and led me to understand that Gretchen was right and I needed to do more in-depth reporting, which, in case you ever work for him, you should know is what he always says.

Do you know **Adam Grant**? If you're a member of the elite reading this acknowledgments section because your name might be here, you probably do. He spent an hour brainstorming interesting things to do for this book, all of which involved cooperation and experiments and stuff I didn't pull off. But he sure did inspire me.

Sitcom-writing genius **Ben Wexler**, wise *Wreck-It Ralph* writer **Phil Johnston**, thoughtful author **Chris Noxon**, and gifted actor **John Staley** labored through an early draft and gave me storytelling advice and encouragement, which was not warranted, but was appreciated.

You know how jokes in Hollywood movies and sitcom pilots are punched up by professionals? Why can't that be done for books? Lots of good reasons, it turns out. I tried it anyway. Several good jokes in this book were written by either **Carrie Kemper** (*Silicon Valley*) or **Bryan Paulk** (*Jimmy Kimmel Live!*, *Chelsea*).

Back when this book was an awful memoir, my college friends and professional editors **Ari Richter** and **Romesh Ratnesar** tried to make it better, which cannot have been a pleasant job. Ari would ask Socratic questions such as "What do you want the reader to get from this book?" which is the nicest way to say "This book sucks."

Only knowing boarding-school-educated, Society of Colonial Wars member **Windsor Mann** through his tweets, I was surprised to learn he is a real person with the real given name Windsor Mann. I was even more surprised when the *USA Today* columnist and editor of *The Quotable Hitchens* emailed me an offer to help with my book. He sent me a trove of information about elitism and responded more quickly and often than anyone else in my perpetual, desperate attempts to choose between lame jokes and clarify points. If you need to hire someone, and can afford someone named Windsor Mann, call him immediately.

I wouldn't be writing books about smart-people stuff, or books at all, if not for **Walter Isaacson, Joshua Cooper Ramo**, and **Cyndi Stivers**, who gave me journalism jobs I was in no way qualified for and am still not, even after having done them.

I begged a lot of very smart, busy people to talk to me. Then I cut them out of this book. That's because I didn't know what I was doing. I feel badly about this. Mostly for them, but also for me, because I wrote a lot of unnecessary words. I spent several days with **Elise Loehnen**, the very smart, very kind editor in chief of Goop. **Jean Godfrey June**, Goop's beauty editor, came to my house to teach me about parabens. I met the writer **Anna Blessing** at a Goop event, and she read a bad, early draft of this book and nicely said that it was lacking me, which meant it was boring.

Michael Shermer, the founder of the Skeptics Society and editor of *Skeptic* magazine, spent time on the phone with me lamenting people's refusal to accept scientific facts. **Brett Weinstein**, the biology professor who was kicked out of Evergreen State College for refusing to leave campus when it declared a Day of Absence from white people, and **Alice Dreger**, the former professor at Northwestern's medical school and the author of *Galileo's Middle Finger*, taught me about how the far-left on campus has come to distrust science because it's been historically used to justify racism and sexism. I failed to fit that stuff in, too.

Phil Stutz, author of *The Tools* and *Coming Alive*, gave me a free therapy session about how to get past writer's block and be brave enough to write something serious. I was not that brave, but at least I wrote something.

You would think that if people are in the dedication you don't also have to put them in the acknowledgments, but that is not a wise way to think about your personal relationships. My lovely wife, **Cassandra Barry**, put up with my self-hatred as I worked on this book, and let me write about her. My sister, **Lisa Stein-Browning**, read drafts and spurred me to finish with the wise words, "No one is going to read it anyway," which is what you need to believe in order to write well. My sweet, sensitive son, **Laszlo Stein**, kept giving me joke ideas. I feel badly for cutting the one about me being racist toward cats.

When Nick Bilton came to pick me up one evening, Laszlo came outside to see Nick's Porsche, which he parked down the street. Nick and I started talking at my doorstep, got distracted, and left without showing the car to him.

"What?" Cassandra asked Laszlo after he told her he hadn't seen the car. "Should I tell him you're mad?"

"No," my son said. "It's his man date. He deserves this. He's been working hard on his book."

He's got the right elite priorities. My son is not a Boat Elite.